AF574406

Underdogs in Overdrive

10 Insanely Great Ideas for the Asian Technopreneur

Dear Larry and Francis —

Enjoy the book - hopefully as much as I enjoyed writing it.

Ilyas

Underdogs in Overdrive

10 Insanely Great Ideas for the Asian Technopreneur

Ilyas Khan

John Wiley & Sons (Asia) Pte Ltd

Singapore New York Chichester

Brisbane Toronto Weinheim

Copyright © 2001 by John Wiley & Sons (Asia) Pte Ltd
Published in 2001 by John Wiley & Sons (Asia) Pte Ltd
All rights reserved.

No part of this publication may be reproduced, stored in a retrieval system or transmitted in any form or by any means, electronic, mechanical, photocopying, recording, scanning or otherwise, except as expressly permitted by law, without either the prior written permission of the Publisher, or authorization through payment of the appropriate photocopy fee to the Copyright Clearance Center. Requests for permission should be addressed to the Publisher, John Wiley & Sons (Asia) Pte Ltd, 2 Clementi Loop, #02-01, Singapore 129809, tel: 65-4632400, fax: 65-4646912, e-mail: enquiry@wiley.com.sg.

This publication is designed to provide accurate and authoritative information in regard to the subject matter covered. It is sold with the understanding that the publisher is not engaged in rendering professional services. If professional advice or other expert assistance is required, the services of a competent professional person should be sought.

The author will donate all net proceeds from royalties to a charity that has been established for the purchase of technology equipment for schools and orphanages in rural parts of Asia.

Other Wiley Editorial Offices

John Wiley & Sons, Inc., 605 Third Avenue, New York, NY 10158-0012, USA
John Wiley & Sons Ltd, Baffins Lane, Chichester, West Sussex PO19 1UD, England
John Wiley & Sons (Canada) Ltd, 22 Worcester Road, Rexdale, Ontario M9W 1L1, Canada
John Wiley & Sons Australia Ltd, 33 Park Road (PO Box 1226), Milton, Queensland 4064, Australia
Wiley-VCH, Pappelallee 3, 69469 Weinheim, Germany

Library of Congress Cataloging-in-Publication Data

Khan, Ilyas.
Underdogs in overdrive: 10 insanely great ideas for the Asian technopreneur / Ilyas Khan.
p. cm.
Includes index.
ISBN 0-471-47907-1 (pbk. : alk. paper)
1. Information technology—Asia. 2. Information technology—Economic aspects—Asia
3. Electronic commerce—Asia 4. Entrepreneurship—Asia. 5. New business enterprises—Asia. I. Title.

HC415.I55 K47 2001
658.8'4—dc21

00-068518

Typeset in 12/18.3 points, New Caledonia by Linographic Services Pte Ltd
Printed in Singapore by Craft Print International Ltd.
10 9 8 7 6 5 4 3 2 1

Contents

What you can do, or dream that you can do, begin it; boldness has genius, power and magic in it.

— Goethe

Dream your dream, work damn hard, free your mind, and have a hell of a lot of fun along the way!

— Johnny Chan, CEO and co-founder, techpacific.com

Preface

The planning and writing of this book has been a very enjoyable experience for me. The cartoons by Trigg, the attitudes of my co-contributors, and the overall approach that I have taken reflect my fundamental belief that we should always aspire to blend our "vocation" with our "avocation" (a tip of the hat to Robert Frost).

I have seen a huge upsurge in talent and entrepreneurship stemming from start-up technology, Internet and Web businesses across the Asian region since starting techpacific.com in 1998. At the same time, I have noted the dearth of written material targeted specifically at start-up and young companies in this new sector of the economy, and which is relevant to this part of the world. This book therefore arose out of my own search for relevant reading material during the period when Johnny Chan (the co-founder of techpacific.com) and I were starting to build our company.

There are shelves full of self-help and "how to" books with an American or European focus, but relatively few books have been written in Asia with Asian-based technology businesses in mind. This is perhaps not surprising, since, historically, Asian talent has had to migrate across the Pacific to the West Coast of the United States, and into Silicon Valley, in order to obtain high-level funding and build successful businesses. Access to "smart" money in the Asia-Pacific region has been restricted to a few lucky breaks, as the venture capital marketplace in general has been more interested in avoiding risk by leaving true start-up funding to private individuals.

The changes that are taking place today in the way capital is allocated in Asia, and the deregulation of markets that will ultimately allow technology companies to find a listing in this region rather than always having to look toward US investors and the NASDAQ market, mean that this will no longer be the case. With the establishment of the Growth Enterprise Market, or GEM (Hong Kong), MESDAQ (Malaysia), SESDAQ (Singapore), and KOSDAQ (Korea), the "route to market" has suddenly become more visible.

Even at the depressed prices of some of the companies that have gone public, entrepreneurs who have taken advantage of this new route to a broader range of locally based investors now have the opportunity for growth that was not available in the past.

It is clear, therefore, that despite the obviously inflated values that some businesses have achieved in the past year or so, and despite an equal or greater number of spectacular failures, a confluence of circumstances has occurred that has changed the landscape for Asian technology entrepreneurs forever. This book is about taking advantage of those changes.

One of the most fundamental changes is the fact that risk capital, or venture capital as it is more commonly called, is more widely available to Asian entrepreneurs within Asia. It's my conviction that an enormous amount of wealth and value will be created in Asia's tech sector and that a good part of this wealth will be created by Asian entrepreneurs who obtain funding from Asian-based investors.

It is also my hope that this book will enable the reader to relate to the reality of doing business here in Asia. It is intended to be the forerunner of what I hope will be a whole new category of publications that are relevant for the new economy in Asia. It is therefore aimed mainly at those people who need somewhere to start in their quest to find relevant information.

I hope that the book will be a source of inspiration for those who are making the truly momentous decisions that need to be taken when great companies first come to life.

In addition to being what I believe is a first book for Asian net-entrepreneurs, or "technopreneurs," this book is about a set of values. It's about openness, transparency, and being upfront with disclosure. It is these qualities which the technology sector (and, indeed, any business endeavor) requires of its winners.

The "lessons" contained here are derived from what I have learned while building my own technology company, as well as from investing in and alongside such winners as Netease, Softbank, and News Corp. The lessons can clearly be identified and articulated by reference to those experiences.

This book is also clearly derived from my close involvement in looking at business plans as part of my job at techpacific.com. Nothing works better than having to implement your values every day of your working life! Since starting techpacific.com, I must have looked at hundreds of business plans, and at the time of writing we at techpacific.com have invested in over thirty-five companies. More importantly, we have been able to help early stage ventures to raise over US$250 million of extremely valuable equity capital for a variety of Asian technology companies. Some of the businesses we have helped or invested in were no more than concepts when we were first introduced to them, and the fact that they have subsequently grown to become substantial businesses in their own right provides us with a great deal of pleasure.

Many of the businesses and people that I have used to illustrate certain points (especially in the "Once upon a time ..." sections) are taken from my experience at techpacific.com, and some of the companies are thus our partners. This makes the "lessons" more relevant than mere theory.

One of my personal role models, Guy Kawasaki (who still runs garage.com — www.garage.com), in his book *Rules for Revolutionaries*, ends his final chapter with a quotation which I think is very appropriate and which I would like to use at the very beginning of my own modest contribution to the world of business writing:

> *The ideas I stand for are not mine. I borrowed them from Socrates. I swiped them from Chesterfield. I stole them from Jesus. And I put them in a book.*
>
> — *Dale Carnegie*

The chapters in this book stand alone and can be read in any order. Each chapter covers one of the ten "insanely great ideas" or guidelines that I believe Asian technopreneurs need to apply if their businesses are to become winners. The chapters start with an explanation of the guideline, along with quotations and cartoons that illustrate the point being made.

The explanations are followed by a number of exercises. These suggested routines are aimed at developing the broad purpose of this book, which is to help aspiring technopreneurs to appreciate the sheer scale of what can be achieved, and to become inspired to achieve their own dreams.

Finally, I have used a wide variety of true accounts from my own experience, or from the experience of well-known entrepreneurs and businessmen, in the "Once upon a time ..." sections.

The accompanying CD-ROM contains all the text, along with hyperlinks to all the companies mentioned in the text and high-resolution copies of the cartoons. There is also an amusing flash-based cartoon created by Velocity9 (www.velocity9.com) that I hope you will enjoy.

If you would like clarification of any point in this book, or if you simply want to take issue with something I have written, please email me. I look forward to receiving feedback from you.

Ilyas Khan
ilyas@techpacific.com
January 2001

Acknowledgments

I owe a huge debt of gratitude to the many people who helped me to complete this work. Among them are:

Johnny Chan, my partner and co-founder at techpacific.com, without whom the book would be just a collection of my favorite sayings. Johnny is a great leader, and living proof that having a positive attitude is worth more than anything else.

David Ketchum, my agent and my friend, without whom this book would have remained a few hundred pages of digital bits on my hard drive. David is also the founder of a great company called Upstream Limited. You can find out more about David and his team at www.upstreamasia.com.

Nick Wallwork, my publisher at John Wiley & Sons in Singapore, who had the courage to sign me when I was still thinking of putting down my ideas in a series of newspaper articles. God bless you, Nick. Also, in the same context, Janis Soo, my editor at John Wiley, and Robyn Flemming, the copyeditor, who helped turn my scattered sentences into coherent prose. It is impossible for someone like me, an inexperienced author, to conceive of completing a book unless angels like Robyn and Janis do their jobs.

Robert Owen, my friend and the chairman of techpacific.com, whose support and faith in me gave me the initial courage to leap into the future being heralded by the "new" economy.

Ali, Stephen, Joey, Yuda, Kenyon, and Shahzad — the original dream team back at techpacific.com 'version 0.1.'

The various "invested partners" and "mentors" who have been inspirational during the past few years. You know who you are, and my eternal thanks go to you.

My colleagues at techpacific.com, who have my deepest respect for being responsible for taking an idea and creating a top-class business.

And finally, Teresa, my muse. I promise not to write another book for quite some time!

Introduction

In late 1998, I was fortunate to be able to start working in a business that I co-founded with my friend, Johnny Chan. This book isn't a history of that company, techpacific.com, nor is it a treatise on how to build an "insanely great business"; rather, it's a book that has been inspired by the lessons I have learned during the wonderful journey we have been on since that time.

A second inspiration for this book was a belief that was central to the creation of techpacific.com, and which remains a motivating factor each day when I get up and go to work. That inspiration is my belief in the absolute enormity of the opportunity that lies ahead of us in the next decade in Asia. An additional conviction is that much of the wealth and opportunity that will be created through the continuing technological revolution will be due to the hard work and innovation of Asian entrepreneurs.

Never in the history of business has the "underdog" had so much access to the essential ingredients for building a successful business. If you believe that the business-building opportunities afforded by the technology and Internet revolution have run their course, then you are making as much of a mistake as those who leaped blindly into the technology sector without adequate preparation and with the sole intention of making a "quick buck."

The next decade will provide us all with the opportunity to develop our entrepreneurial spirit and, for those who decide to take the plunge, a real chance at being a winner.

I have maintained for the past few years that there will be no greater source of wealth creation in Asia in the first decade of the new millennium than the technology sector. Not banking, not property, not automobiles, not petrochemicals, not stockbroking — nor any other sector.

Technology will lead the way, and Internet- and Web-based businesses will be at the core of this wealth-creating phenomenon, the size and scale of which is unprecedented.

Probably the most widely understood measure of difference between the "new" and "old" types of economic model is speed — speed of change, speed of thought, and speed of action. In many respects, the qualities of speed underlie a number of the ideas presented in this book. While entrepreneurs who are involved in business areas that might be seen as "old" economy might also benefit from the guidelines set out here, for those who have jumped into the "deep end" of the "new" economy pool, these guidelines might be considered fundamental building blocks.

The volatility of the stock markets and the weakness of the Internet sector for much of the period since April 2000 have not swayed me from this view. In fact, the correction in the secondary markets such as NASDAQ, and the near collapse of regional markets such as Hong Kong's Growth Enterprise Market, have deepened my faith in the enormous opportunity that lies ahead of us. This volatility has required investors, entrepreneurs, and corporations to become more realistic in their expectations and more selective in the choices they make.

In terms of technology as we see it in practical terms, the changes that will affect us all in the next decade will be greater and more profound than the changes of the past decade. For example, look around you at the gadgets and tools that you have come to depend on in your business, such as the telephone and computers. Sure, they have become more efficient over the last five years or so, but if you were to compare a photograph of your office set-up taken five years ago with one taken today, not a lot will have changed. Over the next few years, the changes will be much more profound and much more obvious, and will be measured in exponential terms. Your Palm Pilot (or other personal device that stores telephone numbers, allows for the taking of short notes, and maybe stores a few games) and telephone will almost certainly be one device, and wireless access will dominate all types of communication.

These changes, and others that are not yet apparent, will be global; and parallel developments in the way in which capital is allocated across markets other than the United

States will spur wealth creation and opportunities unlike anything we have yet witnessed.

It is my deep conviction that some of the brightest thinkers and smartest people live and work here in Asia. I believe that the innovation and enterprise that will be unleashed by Asian entrepreneurs will be unprecedented in history. This wave of success will be stimulated by the opportunities created by the changes that will happen in technology, and the success of these new entrepreneurs and business people will breathe life into the business environment as a whole.

This book aims to provide tomorrow's winners with the basic principles with which to fight the inevitable battle for leadership and success. These guidelines can be used today as the entrepreneurs of the "new" economy build the companies that will become household names tomorrow, and which will generate growth throughout the economy as a whole. The billionaires of the next two decades (and mark my words, there are dozens in the pipeline) will find this manifesto of e-business principles to be an essential part of their preparation.

1

Walk the Walk

In the arena of human life the honors and the rewards fall to those who show their good qualities in action.

— *Aristotle*

Being a winner in the Asian technology space requires breaking all the old "rules." No one can hope to be a leader in the game unless they are willing and able to create a winning formula that starts with themselves.

When great companies are created by entrepreneurs in the hot-bed of technological innovation that is Silicon Valley, the first question that is asked by potential backers is whether the founder is for real. By this, they usually mean: "Will this guy walk the walk, and not just talk the talk?"

I believe that this is no different in Asia, and hence "walking the walk" is the first of my ten guidelines or principles for the Asian technopreneur.

In fact, in the fast-changing world of the Internet space in Asia's resurgent economies, whether the founder is walking the walk is often the most important question that will be asked. It's certainly the first question that I ask at techpacific.com when evaluating an application from a potential investee company. It's therefore the first — and most important — question you should ask yourself as an aspiring technopreneur.

So, what is walking the walk?

Walking the walk means that the founder of a business will follow through with the concept and the business plan. It requires the entrepreneur to take the lead. When done effectively, it exposes the simple fact that it's not good enough for a founder of a technology business simply to expound a philosophy and then retire to the boardroom.

Being a "hands-off" promoter doesn't work in the new millennium; even the most well-connected (in the traditional sense) leaders will fail if they don't walk the walk.

Walking the walk also means leading from the front. It means doing what you say you will do, day in and day out. It can mean working without reward for months on end — and being prepared to do so. It means doing the photocopying, making the coffee, turning out the lights, washing the coffee cups, and putting paper in the printer.

It means establishing principles, and then sticking to them. It means doing everything in your power to deliver your business plan and create value for your stakeholders.

It means that when the dust settles, you can look back with pride at the milestones you have achieved and be able to say, with conviction, that you were a part of every one of them, because you never asked anyone to do something that you yourself wouldn't do.

In order to burn out, a person needs to have been on fire at one time.

— *Ayala Pines*

Exercises

Remembering your promises

There are hundreds of promises that you must have made to people who have helped you. You may have unwittingly broken dozens of them, sometimes for reasons that you can't remember or because of events that were outside your control.

Take some time to write down a few of the promises that you can remember having made and then broken. Write them down in simple language that will help you to remember the context.

Now write down the positive consequences that could have occurred had you kept those promises.

Action is character, right? What a person does is what he is, not what he says.

— *Syd Field*

Putting yourself in your investors' shoes

Next time you go to raise capital (or the first time, if you've yet to start your business) and you start evangelizing, ask your potential investor if he can do you a special favor.

If he agrees, ask him to take off his shoes. Then go around to his side of the table and try them on.

Show him that you understand that part of what will help you succeed is that you are prepared to step into the other person's shoes.

If he doesn't immediately call security and have you evicted, this is a good sign!

Maintaining a positive attitude

In walking the walk, you need to ensure that you adopt and maintain a positive attitude. The whole world likes people who are positive, and who smile and act with the conviction that fate is on their side. Since I believe that we make our own luck, this exercise should be a normal consequence of walking the walk.

Make sure that you exhibit this positive attitude to those with whom you come into contact. Negativism isn't appropriate for the successful tech business leader in this new world! The next time someone gives you a hard time or is cynical about what you are doing, meet them with positive energy and see how easily such small setbacks and petty cynicism can be dealt with.

Once upon a time...

When Johnny Chan and I co-founded techpacific.com, one of our early rules was that we would always try to walk the walk. This meant a number of different things for us, but most of all, it meant that we would put our own hard-earned capital to work and invest not only in our company, but also in the deals that we "qualified" as part of our M^3 business. The M^3 business is in many ways the core of our activity at techpacific.com and represents a new way of allocating capital to talented entrepreneurs in Asia. It is also my belief that we couldn't have built our business as rapidly and as independently as we have without adhering to this philosophy.

In the M^3 program, we invite businesses from all over Asia to approach us about obtaining funding from some of the most influential investors in technology on a global basis, including techpacific.com itself. (Visit our website at www.techpacific.com to learn more about the M^3 program.)

By doing this, we are walking the walk: we aren't asking our investors and supporters to do something that we ourselves wouldn't do.

This is a principle that Johnny and I have continued to apply without compromise. We have promised each other that at the first sign of weakness, the other will promptly douse the offender with a bucket of freezing water. Luckily, we've both avoided that fate so far!

Getting back to the story ...

Pretty soon, after two or three months in the business, we found that we were close to running out of cash. This was a time when raising capital for a raw Internet start-up was extremely difficult. At the same time, we had the good fortune to have unearthed some great deals, including our first "China" deal in the form of Netease (www.netease.com) and our first e-commerce transaction in the form of Bigsave (www.bigsave.com). This good fortune was due in part to the old adage about being in the "right place at the right time" being true for us, but it also stemmed from our ability to leverage our connections from our past careers.

In order to close these early deals, we needed to "step up to the plate" with an amount of capital which, though modest, was considerably more than our company possessed at that time. In our chosen field, and given our early status as a start-up, it wasn't enough to try and achieve success by being smart. We had to be able to access some capital, and our investors would want to see some evidence of "skin in the game" before they would commit meaningfully and co-invest alongside us.

Despite these problems posed by techpacific.com having very limited capital, we committed to the deal and "walked the walk" by putting our own money on the line. When it mattered, we put our hands into our own pockets and made sure that we carried through with our personal and corporate commitments. At the time that the opportunity was presented to techpacific.com, the company had about US$700,000 in the bank, and investing over a third of that capital into Netease was a gutsy thing to do.

Even with our own capital (US$275,000), we needed more money. The prospect of raising further capital for the deals was scary, as our track record as a business was limited at best. (We were still just over six months old.) Johnny and I invested our own cash to supplement the firm's investment, and we found, to our great surprise and relief, that when we went to our two original outside shareholders (Regent Pacific and Tekbanc), they both also stepped up to the plate without hesitation.

In retrospect, I believe that their confidence in us was due in large part to the fact that they were impressed by our adherence to the principle of walking the walk. I have spoken to both these investors (who are still shareholders today) about those early deals, and I am absolutely convinced that their faith in our judgment wouldn't have been as great were it not for our actions in matching our words as individuals and as a business.

Since those early days, we have been able to broaden the application of this same philosophy in other ways that have reinforced the commitment that we show to the business that we created.

Another example of the way in which we walk the walk is the investment in our company by Softbank (www.softbank.com). As part of the investment process that was followed by Softbank, we decided that we would show our own faith in the company by investing as much as possible on a personal basis in the same funding round. We extended the invitation to all our staff, and we were staggered when every single member of the team decided to walk the walk and invest in the company at the same price as Softbank. At the time, many of us were on low (in my case zero) salaries, and so investing our savings was a big statement.

This practice of investing in our company has stayed with us: all of my colleagues in the management team, and most of the people in the firm as a whole, have walked the walk each time we have raised capital from outside investors. This included our Initial Public Offering (IPO), when, during turbulent market conditions, over 10% of the shares being offered were subscribed to by members of our staff! Hiring our current team is one of the best things we've done.

There are some other things we do at techpacific.com that exemplify this approach of walking the walk in both a personal and a corporate sense:

1. We never ask an investee or an investor to contemplate doing something we ourselves wouldn't do.
2. We never qualify a company into Nirvana unless we are prepared to invest in it ourselves. Nirvana is our online exchange where institutional and corporate investors in technology are presented with investment

opportunities. You can learn more about this process, and the way in which we manage Nirvana, by visiting our website at www.techpacific.com.

3. We took vastly under-market salaries — in some cases, no salaries at all — in order to get the business off the ground. Johnny and I led from the front in this regard, and in the first year or so of our existence as a company, our employees were committed enough to withstand offers of significant salaries from our competitors. There is no doubt that one of the reasons we were successful is that we operated a very generous option program. As we have grown more successful, and as we have now become a listed company, we have been able to increase the salary scales so that, whilst we may not pay at the top of the market, we certainly don't pay at the bottom either.
4. We enforce absolute transparency in all aspects of our communication with team members. Many people have difficulty with the concept of wide-ranging transparency. A common point that is made is that it might be acceptable to be transparent with a small team, but what happens when a company grows? My response is simply to point out to those people that the rules of transparency with corporations have changed so quickly that assumptions about the relationship between a company's size and its ability to be transparent are now outdated. Intranets, the

Internet itself, the immediacy of the media, and the working habits of companies that are involved in technology and the Internet militate against opaqueness. Any company that wants to retain its most talented staff will find that transparency is a necessity. This is even more the case in early-stage companies, and is a principle that all entrepreneurs would do well to heed.

5. We provide all team members with real equity participation, and not just gestures in terms of high-priced options. I have seen many companies face difficulty as they grow when they try to "cheat" on this point by making high-sounding gestures about company-wide options schemes that amount to small fractions and percentages of equity. The time to be generous with equity options is in the early stages of a company's development, when you want your employees to act as if they are your co-owners.
6. No one in our team has a separate office — it's open plan all the way. This encourages easier communication and further enforces accountability. I haven't been near a closed office since I started techpacific.com, and my experience has taught me that the benefits of working alongside my colleagues far outweigh any disadvantages.

Not all of the above may be relevant for your business, but the spirit behind the adoption of these practices is what makes us not only "talk the talk," but also "walk the walk."

2

Live the Dream

Running a technology business in the 21st Century is a bit like dreaming with both eyes open.

— Robert Owen, chairman, techpacific.com

Dreams, by definition, are always personal, and very few people have the ability to convince others to share or experience their own dream. The short history of the technology revolution in global terms has already established that the real winners are those leaders who can take a personal dream and extend it to a wider audience. In effect, they help their colleagues to "share" the experience.

In 21st century Asia, and in the tech world, you must "live the dream" in a different and more immediate way if you are going to be a winner. In the wired world of the new media age, a dream that spawns a tech business needs to be displayed and exemplified again and again and again. Ad infinitum.

Founders should eat, sleep, breathe, and play their dream. It isn't enough just to reduce your dream to a twenty-minute slide presentation. It's not enough that your team and your colleagues are aware of your dream just while they're at work during the day. You need to be able to transcend what might be considered normal human boundaries and show, in all your actions, how your dream has affected you and how it will affect others.

Building a successful tech business requires an evangelism on the part of the founder that was rarely required in business in the "old" economy. This may sound like an exaggeration, but I believe that we haven't yet reached the stage where building an Internet business can be equated with starting a bakery or building another shopping center. The reasons for the need for greater evangelism are rooted in the fact that times of change require a greater effectiveness of communication, and being "evangelistic" about your new business will create energy and a focus that will enable people to understand what you are doing.

Evangelism and a belief in oneself can't exist on their own, without other values and disciplines. But I believe that being an evangelist and a believer in your business and your product is a requirement that must not be compromised.

Problems relating to the business environment in Asia, where the development of the Internet has lagged the rest of the world, mean that technopreneurs have to live out their dream through a manifestation of themselves. In fact, the economic crisis that has only recently abated in many parts of Asia has been instrumental in bringing to the fore the realization of how damaging closed markets and nepotism can be in terms of stifling competition and progress. It's my view that the economic crisis has ultimately provided a great opportunity for young entrepreneurs, because it has allowed some of the vested interest groups to become less influential. This fact has been positively enhanced by the timing of the technology revolution, and the opportunities that are being created by the confluence of circumstances that I have described above (and which also led me to write this book) may never be repeated.

Living your dream means that you are able to show how your Web business will affect all aspects of your life, and the lives of others. When Sabeer Bhatia, one of the early heroes in Asian Internet entrepreneurship, built Hotmail (www.hotmail.com), he knew how his dream would affect the world. He managed to live his dream; in so doing, he convinced Microsoft to pay him hundreds of millions of dollars for Hotmail, which has continued to affect the lives of millions of people around the world and remains a leader in Web-based email.

Sabeer's story has been told many times and has been influential in inspiring venture capitalists as well as entrepreneurs. The story of how Sabeer (who now lives in India) started Hotmail and managed to attract venture capital (from Draper Fisher Jurvetson) at a time when the mass appeal of the Internet was in its infancy, and of how he negotiated with Microsoft (defying the advice of his backers and investors to sell at a price many times below his eventual negotiated agreement), has become part of Internet folklore. MBA courses and "how to" books have taken liberties with what must have been a considerably more difficult passage than we might imagine. My use of the example is really to highlight the way in which the story of success is the story of individuals like Sabeer Bhatia, who is really no different from you or me — and he has lived his dream.

Still on the subject of India, the guys over at Satyam Computer Systems (www.satyam.com) and their subsidiary

Satyam Infoway Limited (www.sify.com) have been dreaming for many years about mass Internet access to Indian homes. In fact, they started to build their dream at a time when most people weren't even aware of the potential of the ISP business in monopoly-controlled India. They persevered, and were committed to subsidizing their earnings in order to build their dream. The markets have finally realized and have now rewarded them for their foresight. In many ways, the founders and management of Satyam have been able to display their dream to a broader audience that is now participating in it alongside them.

This adoption of a dream, and the "buy-in" of the early employees of a company, needs massive amounts of discipline. The market for connectivity in India is still very difficult to make any headway in, and though the size of the business that Satyam have built is obvious to all, the obstacles that hindered their progress in the early days cannot easily be appreciated. The pursuit of their dream has led to Satyam Computer Systems being one of the largest companies in India.

Most successful technopreneurs have realized that, in the Internet age, the only capital that really matters is intellectual capital. Companies and businesses such as Hotmail and Satyam have taught us that our dreams are the product of a combination of our emotions and our intellect, and living our dream means that we create our own currency.

Intellectual capital — ideas as money, money as ideas — is today the real currency of the business world. This capital is more than technical knowledge or bits and bytes of data.

— *Mark Bryan,* The Artist's Way at Work

Successful technopreneurs will keep Mark Bryan's quote close to their hearts as they take the first steps in setting up their business. Even today, with techpacific.com being a listed company, and with a brand that is recognized and respected across our core markets in Asia, Johnny and I walk into our office each day with a vision that we know has yet to be fulfilled. Our dream continues to inspire us and everything that we do, and everything we communicate to our colleagues and our partners is based on this fundamental ideal. In this way, a large part of our success has been our ability to stay focused on our dream and to allow the people around us to understand and share in the vision.

In regard to living one's dream, I am reminded of a visit that I made early in 2000 to the Cisco Systems campus, in Silicon Valley. The sheer energy of this company, which is one of the largest enterprises in the world in market capitalization terms, is only one of the things that impressed me during the visit. The other thing was the way in which employees, from top to bottom, have "bought into" the dream. John Chambers and his senior colleagues have helped to create an operating culture that is almost religious in its devotion to the Cisco cause, and it's the existence of this "living dream" that has helped to sustain the growth and market leadership of this admirable corporation.

As the manager now of a company with over 100 direct and indirect employees, I ask myself how the Cisco phenomenon works. The answer is actually very simple, but like most simple things that work at this scale, it takes real application and hard work to succeed.

The answer is focus and communication. Employees at Cisco understand why they go to work each day. I have a friend who is a senior member of the management staff, and his comments to me bear repeating here:

> *When I first came to work at Cisco, I thought I knew what we wanted to do. Within a week of being here, I knew that I would probably not want to leave. Now, five years later, I'm as eager to come to work each day as on the day I joined.*
>
> *My colleagues, my senior managers, and virtually all the people around me are believers in our mission statement, and we are constantly told about events in our company that I know for sure would pass by most people in other corporations.*

This friend is a wealthy individual because of his work at Cisco. I don't know if he will retire from there or move on, but I do know that a large part of his devotion is due to the fact that Cisco communicates its mission and its dream again and again and again.

This point about employee retention is also drummed home in a recently published book by David Bunnell, called *Making the Cisco Connection: The Story Behind the Real Internet Superpower*. In a chapter entitled "The Benevolent Predator," Bunnell discusses the superb track record of Cisco in keeping its employees, and makes the comment: "Chambers' philosophy on employee retention is that Cisco tells employees up front what Cisco's plans are because trust is everything. Employees find it hard not to fall in love with Cisco stock options. New employees become part of future acquisition teams. If it works for them, it sure can work for you!"

Exercises

Dreaming with both eyes open

There is often a big difference between dreaming and hoping. For those of you who manage to live your dream, the differences will disappear, and your hopes and dreams will become one.

It's true what they say: attitude and frame of mind count for a lot.

What do you *dream* of doing this time next year?

Write down a quick answer. A scrawl will do — enough to remind you what you believe to be your dream.

Now, what do you *hope* to be doing this time next year? Is your hope the same as your dream?

> *Dreams and play have to do with developing the new, whereas maturity, like it or not, has a lot to do with maintaining the status quo.*
>
> — *George Vaillant*

I really like this quotation, and I often use it to help my colleagues to continue to focus on their "creative" side, not just their business side.

Expressing yourself

Can you describe one of your dreams to someone else, maybe a friend or a colleague, and be comfortable that you have managed to express the essence of what you experienced during the dream?

Capturing the essence of a dream, being able to describe it and feeling convinced that the listener has actually understood, isn't a simple task.

Articulating your dreams

Try to remember a dream. Making one up won't work here, so try to remember an actual dream you've had. (Bad luck to those of you who don't remember your dreams!)

Choose someone you can talk to, but not someone who is very close to you. Go and tell them about the dream.

Did they get it?

Being moved by someone else's dream

Finally for this chapter, visit a video store and try to find a video with footage of the famous speech made by Martin Luther King in 1963 that called: "I have a dream ..."

If, after listening to this speech, you remain unmoved by it, then don't bother trying to live your dream. You might be able to build a business, but it won't be as brilliant as it might have been if you had the emotional capability to be moved by another person's dream.

However, if listening to the speech moves you in an emotional, tangible way (I was moved to tears when I heard and understood what King was saying), then welcome to the club. You now know that you possess at least one of the essential attributes for building a successful business.

Once upon a time...

The guys who now manage Chinadotcom, one of Asia's first NASDAQ companies in the Internet space (www.china.com), include a hard core of people who created and ran a successful Web-building business called The Web Connection (TWC).

Ian Henry, who was a founder of TWC (part of Chinadotcom) and is now a sought-after and admired dot.com guru in Asia, remembers when the glamor was a distant dream. For years before the Internet became as popular and glamorous as it is today, the team at TWC worked hard just to stay afloat.

Ian told me once of the bucket that used to occupy a corner of his office, and which was often called into action to catch the water dripping from a leaking roof. He and his colleagues, including Peter Hamilton who is now chief operating officer at Chinadotcom, worked hard to move his "vision" from such humble beginnings to the success that Chinadotcom is today. But his story isn't just about finding the ability to create success and transform a company that worked out of an office with a leaking roof into a multi-billion dollar organization.

Things have changed, of course, but the "proof of concept" for Ian and his colleagues was a dream that they were able to nurture and eventually realize. Ian's story might well be replicated in the traditional economy, which has been full of stories of hard-working business people who have been able to transform their fortunes. However, in the case of Chinadotcom and Ian Henry, the real lesson is the ability of this technology entrepreneur to live his dream from the very beginning.

When TWC was started, the notion of a Web design and services company becoming a multi-million dollar business in Hong Kong was scoffed at by most people. I'm not just talking here about the value of the company, but the amount of revenues that they generate. This scale, however, was very much a part of Ian's vision, and he has spoken of the way in which they built their company around a vision and a dream that was shared initially by the employees, and ultimately by a diverse group of stakeholders.

There are any number of such stories in the United States, but here in Asia we need our own role models who can affirm the value of living one's dream. Ian Henry, Peter Hamilton, and The Web Connection team are just the first of many such examples that exist here, and they should serve to inspire you to live your own dream.

Another great example of someone who has lived their dream has emerged in Hong Kong in the form of David Loiterton and his Internet company, gogo.com (www.gogo.com). I first met David when he was running BMG Music Asia's business, based out of Hong Kong, with a music publishing empire that was one of the most extensive and influential in the Asian market, covering the whole "waterfront" from Japan and Australia to China and India.

When David came to "pitch" his idea to techpacific.com, he said something that I still associate with gogo.com. He said: "The Internet was made for music, and music is ideal for the Internet."

David clearly nurtured a dream about the way in which the infrastructure and the content of the Internet would undergo profound changes, and he believed that music across a mass Asian market would be one of the areas where the changes would be the most significant and long-lasting.

David's views were based not only on MP3 technology (which he has been quoted as saying is only a passing phase), but also on the secure delivery of music across the Internet in a digital form that is acceptable to and economical for the music companies and the consumer.

As a leading executive in the music industry, David and his wife Nikki certainly lived a comfortable life. Traveling business class and first class, and occupying a luxurious flat in Hong Kong's Mid-Levels, David was on a fast track that would lead to a position of seniority in one of the world's largest music companies. In addition, as we learned when we asked around the industry, David enjoyed the respect and goodwill of industry players in all of the key markets.

The question was whether he had the courage to jump into the Internet as an entrepreneur, and to risk what he had built over a life-long career.

"Living the dream" is clearly more than a statement of visionary appeal, and David exhibited the strength of purpose to take that dramatic and life-changing decision and to transform himself over a weekend in January 2000 from a leading executive with the security and power of a large global organization behind him, into a young Internet start-up with little more than his dream to propel him forward.

It's still early days, of course, for gogo.com, and David's vision of how the Internet will transform the music business is still being played out across the global markets. In the meantime, gogo.com is busy building a stake in that future, and with a partnership with techpacific.com and a modest amount of capital (probably less than a week's operating budget in BMG) he has built something that is already capturing a great deal of attention.

David Loiterton is living his dream.

3

Aim for the Sky

You don't have guarantees in this world. You've got to take chances.

— Muriel Siebert

Asian business people could hardly be accused of lacking in ambition. In the new century, the new paradigm dismisses old measures, and this is equally true of ambition. Being ambitious in building a technology business will require more courage and daring than during the pre-digital days.

The objectives — indeed, the very meaning and definitions — of success have changed, so that building a tech business in this new age means that no aim can ever be less than sky-high. And at the end of the day, let's face it, you only live once.

> *You don't get to choose how you're going to die. Or when. You can only decide how you're going to live. Now.*
>
> — *Joan Baez*

Any person who achieves success without having a sense of ambition that aims for the sky has just been plain lucky.

When building and communicating a business plan, and evangelizing the dream, the sheer scale of the idea needs to be enforced again and again and again. "Aiming for the sky" is a motivational slogan often used by sportspeople, politicians, and others striving for success in various fields of endeavor. However, for the technopreneur, aiming for the sky has to be a part of their everyday routine and not just a slogan. The rules change so much and so rapidly, that today's sky is easily next week's ground.

Aiming for the sky is also the only way in which the lowest common denominator that proves to be the resting point for team-based organizations can remain set at a high level. In Asia, where talented teams need and demand charismatic leadership in order to stay challenged, aiming for the sky therefore becomes a necessary tool for effective management.

Your team needs to recognize that you will accept nothing less than this lofty ideal, and therefore delivering less is an act of failure.

Aiming for the sky also means having to deal effectively with scorn and disdain. Armchair experts can often have a disproportionate impact on tech businesses. You may be told

that you are being unrealistic, that you won't be able to achieve your objectives. In the short time that we have been operating techpacific.com, we have had our fair share of so-called experts who will risk nothing themselves, but who will criticize everything about us, including our courage and vision. When techpacific.com went public in April 2000, amidst some of the most turbulent conditions that have ever been experienced in stock markets, we were lucky to be supported by some great investors and committed investment banks. However, we also had to endure the criticism of a number of analysts who never even bothered to visit us or research what we did, but just issued pompous-sounding edicts that judged us as if we were another money-losing "me too" portal that would burn out within six months.

Our response to these naysayers was to buckle down and continue to build our business, and to show these people by our actions over a period of time that they were wrong. Needless to say, we are not only surviving but prospering, and many of the same analysts and stockbrokers who criticized us are now suddenly our "best friends"!

I'm sorry to say that this is common human nature. The lesson here for technopreneurs is to continue to be ambitious; don't be put off by people who are ignorant or simply negative because of the prevailing fashion.

As I have said above, the right way to respond to these negative-minded people is to lead from the front and to show by your results that you are operating on a different level.

I would never advise in favor of tackling negative naysayers or armchair critics directly, because they are often not capable of direct dialogue. Remember, if you run your business with the transparency and accessibility that are inherent in the guidelines contained in this book, then you will eventually come out ahead of the game.

You will also learn that in the Internet age, these naysayers are the ones who will have to learn that your aim was correct, and that they underestimated the strength of your vision and your determination.

Exercises

Believing in Nirvana

Nirvana is what we call our online exchange at techpacific.com, but this isn't a plug for the exchange. Nirvana is also the ultimate destination for our souls in classic Buddhist teaching. It's a place that symbolizes peace and the attainment of enlightenment.

This exercise is about projecting your belief in your own version of Nirvana, and not being afraid to communicate it.

Approach someone who is wearing a suit and ask them if they can show you the way to Nirvana. If they don't start shouting for the police, you can assume that they are at least a little intrigued by the question. Complete the exercise by pointing to their heart and telling them that Nirvana exists right there, in their own soul.

While this may not be a practical exercise, it's important to remember that appearances are often deceptive. Asian technopreneurs will always be on the right track if they remember not to be "locked in" by conventional boundaries.

Being ambitious enough in your business plan

If you have a business plan, or a strategy paper for a business that already exists, then take it out and review it — but with only one question in mind: Is the plan ambitious enough? Delete all other thoughts from your mind during this review.

When you can answer the question in the affirmative, and only then, share the plan with your team or your partner.

Ask them the same question: Is the plan ambitious enough? Don't ask them if it's *too* ambitious. Tell them only to focus on whether it is ambitious *enough*.

If they answer in the negative, work with them on the plan until they agree with you that the plan is ambitious enough.

The next day, set yourself the same exercise, and review the plan.

Do this each day for the next three days.

When you have a plan that you believe is ambitious enough, take it to your financier and your shareholders. Before you present the plan, say to them: "Gentlemen, this plan is probably too conservative and I will need your help in making it more ambitious."

When you get the funding you need, buy yourself a celebratory glass of wine (or whatever other drink you prefer) and congratulate yourself on aiming high, then remind yourself never to revert to being overly cautious!

> *Cowards die many times before their deaths; the valiant never taste of death but once.*
>
> — *William Shakespeare,* Julius Caesar

Once upon a time...

When I first started to think about forming techpacific.com, I was introduced to a group of financiers in Europe who were potential partners in our business. One of the senior managers of that company, a former trader who was about my age, exhibited all the signs of wanting to get involved in what we were going to do at techpacific.com, and even expressed an interest in moving to Hong Kong, effectively as a partner in our venture.

After some time, and before we had committed to any deal, I wanted to test his resolve. I took him to lunch and invited him point blank to drop what he was doing and come out to Hong Kong and be a partner in techpacific.com.

The invitation "knocked the stuffing" out of him, and it became obvious that although he talked a good talk, he was unable to carry it off. He was unable to aim for the sky.

During lunch, I even decided to offer him a subsidy in cash if he felt that he would be taking too much of a risk. I told him that I would pay him over the odds to take the chance of a lifetime and build something that was going to be more valuable than anything he had done in his career so far. I did this because I actually thought he could add value, but I also wanted to see if he was, in fact, ambitious or merely "cogitating."

In the end, he lacked the courage even to say "no," and slunk away with a vague promise to get back to me.

His company eventually put up a small portion of the capital needed to finance techpacific.com. Due to some good luck and the hard work of the techpacific.com team, less than a year later their investment was worth considerably more than the rest of their entire company put together. That, as they say, is another story (they are no longer involved in our company, having sold their stake ahead of our IPO), but the trader reminded me of the difference between apparent and true ambition.

Aiming high was a problem for this person, who now has difficulty looking me in the eye when we meet because he knows that he was unable to harness the full power of his imagination.

My partner Johnny has reminded me constantly that a lack of ambition is probably one of the biggest reasons for failure in the Internet business. The flip-side of that same coin is that those technopreneurs who truly reach for the sky are the ones that are more likely to make it.

As a leader of your business or group, you need to show that your expectations are sufficiently high. After all, the greater your belief in yourself, the more likely your colleagues will be able to adopt your expectations.

I also like to point people to Jaewoong Lee, the founder and chief executive officer of Daum Communications (www.daum.co.kr) in Korea and an example of a truly Asian, home-grown visionary. Daum are techpacific.com's partners in our Korean joint venture, and Jaewoong has expressed all the values inherent in the principle of "aim for the sky" by building a world-class business that is a leader in its field.

Daum Communications was constructed on the skill employed by Jaewoong in creating a Korean-language Web-based email system (similar to Hotmail, except using the local Hangul character set instead of English). The initial work was done when the Internet was still just a vague concept for most Koreans and at a time when their country was in the middle of a recession that turned out to be the most severe economic downturn in their history.

As a result, the software was written and developed on a shoestring budget, and the initial numbers of users were limited due to the almost non-existent marketing budget, as well as low Internet penetration rates.

Until Bertelsman (the German media conglomerate) came on the scene in 1998 and provided Daum with its first real capital injection, the story of Daum is one of Jaewoong's ambition being sustained over the many late nights and long days during which his vision never dimmed.

Daum has now become one of the leading Internet destinations in Korea and a leading traffic driver in Asia. Like his neighbor in China, Netease.com, Jaewoong has changed a Web-based email provider into a diversified portal with depth of content and appeal that will be at the forefront of Korea's Internet development.

Daum is now probably the most popular site amongst native Koreans, whilst being the technology company that stands at the top of the list for most international businesses that want a local partner for their Korean roll-out.

Despite now enjoying a status close to that of a rock star in his native Korea, Jaewoong is one of those marvelous entrepreneurs who has not lost his original modesty. He strikes most people who meet him as being someone who has his feet planted firmly on the ground. I have got to know him better since techpacific.com started building a Korean business in a joint venture with Daum, and I have been able to confirm first-hand how well "J.W." has managed to combine spectacular success with a continuing modesty and pragmatism.

Jaewoong Lee, CEO of Daum Communications, aims for the sky.

4

Act with a Heart of Gold

Do all the good that you can, by all the means that you can, in all the ways you can in all the places you can, at all the times you can, to all the people you can, as long as you ever can.

— *John Wesley*

The quotation that starts this chapter is from a prominent Western thinker, but I believe that the Asian way also demands that leaders be compassionate.

The Internet age in Asia imposes a levy on each and every successful business person that is no less demanding than Wesley's maxim. In the new millennium, successful Internet and tech business leaders will operate with a heart of gold, and this essential principle is as important as any of the guidelines outlined in this book that are more obviously business-oriented.

Giving isn't just about making a lot of noise when you write checks for charity once your success is proven. It's about being charitable even when you have little to give.

In the days of the "old" economy, penguin-suited tycoons accompanied by their trophy wives would salve their collective conscience by attending expensive dinners where the act of giving became a spectacle in itself. Hong Kong and Singapore often exhibited the worst examples of this type of giving, where the great and the good fought corporate battles during the day, and mimicked New York and London society in the evenings by attending charity balls which were zealously reported in the local press.

But even for those who have already made it, flashy charity balls and excessive PR-related "giving" will no longer work. Building tech businesses forces you to realize that charity begins at home, and that having a heart of gold has more to do with every act you plan and carry out than with every dollar you donate at charity auctions.

Acting with a heart of gold can be shown in any number of ways. It starts with the demand that you treat others, especially your colleagues, in a way that you would want to be treated yourself. This is one of those phrases that crops up time and time again, and for a good reason — it's true. I have no hesitation in using this phrase, and in urging you always to try and achieve the highest levels of consistency in dealing with people as you build your business.

Businesses that put "flash" ahead of substance are guilty of overlooking this most essential principle. Many Internet start-ups in Asia will go "belly-up" in spectacular fashion because they have been built on flimsy foundations. The act of marketing the sites in order to make the "next" $10 million was more important than the underlying business objectives and dreams for the future.

Many of the entrepreneurs who are behind these failures will have been guilty of the most appalling arrogance and greed, and I'm not sorry to say that I will probably take some delight in witnessing their fall back to earth.

In the process of building your business, you will be called upon to lead from the front time and time again, and acting with a heart of gold will ensure that you won't fail to uphold your end of the bargain and will avoid falling into the "flash before substance" trap. The principle of acting with a heart of gold doesn't just apply to the act of giving in a monetary sense; rather, it means having a conscience that doesn't allow you to mislead or manipulate others. This principle is therefore a perfect corollary to that of walking the walk, since it stands to reason that you can't, or won't, walk the walk if your intentions aren't honorable.

Acting with a heart of gold needn't be a large-scale gesture; acts can be done in small ways, and can be built upon as the companies that you build become successful in their own right. In this circumstance, even if your business fails, if you follow this guideline, you won't fail for the want of compassion.

For example, heart of gold winners will create initiatives within their companies that allow the creation of wealth to be shared with society by allocating options to charity. These options will create value for great causes because, just as the companies themselves become successful, the options will become a valuable commodity helping a good cause. As I explain later in this chapter, we have done this within techpacific.com in a number of ways. Our Karma Trust is an example of our desire to share our success with people in society who are less fortunate, and we have contributed to charity at every step of the way.

If any reader wishes to obtain details of how to create such charitable options, don't hesitate to contact me. I would be pleased to share my views with you in more detail.

At the very start of this book, I outlined my belief that tremendous wealth will be created in Asia during the next decade due to the technology revolution. I am hopeful that this opportunity will spur many entrepreneurs to succeed in their business, but I'm also hopeful that if they follow the principles and guidelines set out here, then acting with a heart of gold will be the way in which the good winners, those with sustainable winning ideas, are distinguished from the "also-rans."

As some of the readers of this book will be aware, proceeds from the royalties of this publication are being given to a charity that will buy computers and communication equipment for schools in rural areas across Asia. This is an act of giving that allows me to continue to practice what I preach, and is a small step toward ensuring that the advance of technology is more meaningful in the longer term.

Asian entrepreneurs in the technology sector who have a "giving attitude" will recycle their success by sharing it with their colleagues. Equity in the business will be given to people at every level of the corporation, and the old Asian adage of elitism in business will be overturned.

These are some of the obvious ways in which you can create and sustain your heart of gold. Sharing your success, being courteous and open to all around you, and creating wealth for a wide cross-section of your employees rather than just a small group of senior managers are all ways in which I suggest you adopt this policy.

"New age" winners won't just have an open-door policy; they'll have no doors. Their hearts of gold will force others within their businesses to adopt open and transparent attitudes. I believe that the winning formula in Asia won't tolerate anything less.

A heart of gold — when giving is as good as receiving.

Exercises

Practicing giving

Donate an amount of money to a worthwhile children's charity. Next month, make another donation.

Don't allow yourself to start feeling smug. If you start to feel smug, increase the amount of your donation.

Think about spending some time working for a cause that is dear to you.

If you work in a start-up, or in fact in any company, then go to your colleagues and insist that a portion of the options that are granted by the company in lieu of cash be reserved for a charity. Then make it happen.

Sticking to the truth

Make a decision that for the next week you won't lie to or mislead anyone intentionally.

At the end of the week, make the decision for a month, and then make it for a year. At the end of the year, email me and let me know how wonderful you feel.

Once upon a time...

I read the quotation below in a book by Laurence Boldt that is still one of my favorites, *Zen and the Art of Making a Living.*

> *Is the system going to flatten you out and deny you your humanity, or are you going to be able to make use of the system for the attainment of human purposes?*
>
> — *Joseph Campbell*

The quotation is an apt way of describing my approach to maintaining the balance that can help you to keep your heart of gold. Amidst the hustle and bustle of building your dream, you and your colleagues will be richer by far if you all act with a heart of gold.

I'm afraid I don't have a true story from our business for this principle. The simple fact is that we are trying hard to create our heart of gold, and we all have a long, long way to go — myself included.

Outside of techpacific.com, I know of many examples of how a heart of gold helps businesses to become bigger and better. The humility of those involved has meant that I cannot use their experience, since it would make them feel as if they were somehow boastful.

I will use this opportunity instead to focus on a few suggestions for entrepreneurs who are starting out with an Internet business in Asia.

1. Consider hiring people with disabilities to work in your business. You'll find that they add more than just functionality.
2. Take a deep breath every morning before you switch on your computer, and think of something you can do better for your colleagues. For example, if you are in the start-up phase, there is little reason why all of the members of the team shouldn't have equity in the business. So if you can identify people who are underrepresented, resolve to do something about it.
3. Each month, take an hour from your schedule and send an email to the team, letting them know what state the business is in. Transparency starts at the top, and you shouldn't assume that people will automatically know what's going on. If you do this often enough, you'll start to share information with all the team members and allow them to participate in more ways than is traditional in an Asian business.
4. Apologize if you make a mistake. If you make mistakes, or if you inconvenience your colleagues, then don't be too arrogant to recognize the fact. This will show that you are concerned about other people, and that you're not just another dot.com jerk. Never shout at your colleagues. If you feel the need to shout, then excuse

yourself, go to the bathroom, and shout at the urinal.

5. If you think someone in your team is underpaid and you have the ability to do something about it, then don't wait until the end of the year. Give them a raise ASAP.
6. Give some of your options or equity to charity. We did this at techpacific.com from the very first day in business, and continue to do so. In fact, since our IPO, Johnny and I have put more options into the Karma Trust from the proceeds of our options program. Again, this is a subject very close to our hearts, and as stated previously, I would be delighted to help others set up a similar charitable option scheme in their own companies.

5

Plan for the Worst

Expect nothing; be prepared for anything.

— Traditional Samurai saying

The pace of change in Asian Web businesses, and in the environment of the Internet, will force even the best-laid plans to be upset, time and time again. Even in Silicon Valley, where the speed of change is supersonic, the most successful entrepreneurs admit that they have managed to achieve success only by allowing for failure. In Asia, where we can expect the rules of business to constantly change, planning for the worst will keep you ahead of the game.

Planning for the worst doesn't mean becoming overly pessimistic or adopting a negative attitude. What it *does* mean is that the skill and verve with which you execute your business plan needs to be tempered with the ability to embrace the most unexpected turns of fate. At techpacific.com, even when we thought we were sailing in clear, calm waters, events have sometimes transpired to remind us that we must always be prepared.

Our IPO process is a wonderful example of how things outside of our control are often the catalyst for contingency planning. Our IPO was conceived during January and February 2000, a time when investors and markets were flying high, and Internet and technology companies were trading at close to their historic all-time highs.

You may recall that this was the period when NASDAQ reached its historic high of over 5000 and tom.com (www.tom.com) went public in Hong Kong amidst scenes of mass greed and hysteria that were flashed across television screens around the world. The IPO of tom.com was one of the most oversubscribed in history, and the shares soared to twelve times their initial price.

Within about ten weeks, this optimism had all but vanished, and NASDAQ lost over 25% (yes, *a quarter of its value*) in just one trading week during April. The impact on our IPO of this enormous change in market conditions was monumental.

Despite the predictions by many people that our deal was going to "fly" into the markets, Johnny Chan and I had made some contingency plans. Because we had prepared for the worst, we were able to handle some of the worst equity markets ever witnessed, and to complete an offering that is still being described by analysts as "unbelievable."

Neither Johnny nor I could have expected that we would have to change our plans as we did, but we were able and willing to do so when the need arose. Johnny often describes our experience at the hands of the market as "humbling," and I share with him the view that we learned more from this single experience than from anything else in our corporate history. We learned that preparing for the worst has to be right up there on the scale of important things to consider.

It's ironic that, in many respects, planning for the best and preparing for the worst is a counter-intuitive business method. The old ways of the pre-digital world in Asia meant that even acknowledging that the worst might happen was to tempt fate. This mind-set is peculiarly Asian, and needs to change. Winning in the Internet age in Asia means being prepared to change a lot of what we think of as traditional business methods and norms. I am surprised by the number of entrepreneurs who react in an extremely negative manner when they are asked to incorporate "contingency" plans in their business roll-out. They seem to believe that the very act of acknowledging the possibility of failure is a sign of weakness. This is clearly not the case, and preparedness is a major part of the successful business person's skill set.

> *Businessmen go down with their businesses because they like the old way so well that they cannot bring themselves to change.*
>
> — *Henry Ford*

When adversity does strike, the best leaders will react as if it is no big deal. Their staff and their colleagues will admire their resilience, but only the entrepreneurs will know that this skill has been acquired at great cost — the cost of acting with conviction in the knowledge that risk can strike at any time.

If you are a technopreneur, then things that you can expect to go wrong include:

- failing to find the right amount of funding;
- competitors who suddenly increase the stakes of the game;
- allies who become rivals;
- staff who defect; and

- market conditions that deteriorate outside of your control.

These are all possibilities that you will need to cater for. Keeping your cool whilst privately expecting these things to occur will help you to savor your successes. Being prepared to deal with problems will mean that you will be able to navigate the inevitable stormy waters better.

In the often random happenstance of business in Asia, planning for these "worst case" scenarios is a mark of the winner, and is a quality that will never be out of fashion.

Exercises

Appreciating forward planning

Take a trip to Bali. Book yourself into a decent hotel, but "forget" to take any beachwear and leave your sun-block at home. Take only enough cash to pay your hotel bills. Put your credit cards in your spare wallet, and leave it in your desk at the office.

Stay for a week.

On your return, you'll appreciate the power of forward planning.

Remind-yourself notes

Write down on a piece of paper "nothing is ever as good as it seems" and on the back write "nothing is ever as bad as it seems."

Carry it with you and read it whenever it's appropriate. (This is something I learnt from my first boss, Nick Roditi, at Schroders in London).

Once upon a time ...

Getting the company started was the easiest thing that Johnny and I did in the first three months of our "entrepreneurial" lives. The rest was a series of mini-disasters that we now look back on and think of as tests of our resolve that helped us with our launch.

These "disasters" also helped to convince us always to have at least one contingency plan. Appreciating that we have a contingency plan is now a sufficient reason for us to feel confident that we can eventually succeed, and we all know the power of positive thinking!

The first problem that hit me, believe it or not, was that the company's original URL was taken from right under my feet. The business plan that we signed off on was for a company that would be called "tech-Asia." Although the URL was available at the time we first came up with the idea, by early 1998, when we actually got around to registering ownership, it was taken.

This may not sound like a disaster, but the sloppiness with which we had approached the matter, and the fear that our fellow seed capital providers would think we were a couple of clowns, sapped my confidence. (Johnny insists he was pretty cool about the whole thing!)

Out of this adversity arose our need to find a new name.

The next three problems were compounding errors that almost caused the good ship techpacific.com to sink at its initial moorings.

As most of our good friends now know, Johnny and I never thought we would end up running the company, so we set about trying to hire a CEO. The first person we thought of was a good friend and ex-colleague, Lisa Wu, and for reasons that now seem entirely plausible, she thought we were nuts. The sad thing is that both Johnny and I actually thought that she would be falling over herself to take the job, so when she turned us down, it was like a slap in the face.

Fresh from this stinging rebuke, we charged into the blind alley of unalloyed optimism, straight into the arms of our next candidate (let's call him Mr. X) who was then working at a large U.S. investment bank. Same pattern, same result, though with greater emotion, since even Mr. X thought he was going to take the job until he was informed otherwise by his family.

On to option three, who shall remain nameless, and who had the good grace at least to pay for the expensive lunch that allowed him to turn us down.

Desperate, and with the pace of new business picking up (we had assumed that we would have a CEO or COO operating by now), we moved on to Philip, who had been my original choice, but who lived in Singapore and would need some convincing to move to Hong Kong.

This time, with a great deal of superstitious huffing and puffing, I really thought I had him in the bag. I even told Johnny that we may need to think of a more technical number two to work with Philip, who was likely to be only slightly more competent with technology than our chairman,

Robert Owen (who, at the time, was still learning how to switch on his laptop without having it hiss at him).

Two weeks later, amid familiar tears of frustration, we resolved that we would just have to do it ourselves and run our own company, since no one else seemed likely to be stupid enough to commit themselves to techpacific.com (the URL that we finally found). And the rest, as they say, is history.

I am indebted to Benny Lee, the founder of Edgetech Limited in Hong Kong, for this next illustration of preparing for the worst.

Benny came to see us in the autumn of 1999 with a plan that would take advantage of his already entrenched position within the retail market of Hong Kong, where he sold and maintained point of sale terminals (POS systems) used by retailers around the world.

Benny has been active in this market for many years now, and those of you who live and work in Hong Kong have probably used one of his many installed systems when paying for your toothpaste at Watson's the drugstore or buying your Coke at 7-Eleven. Benny was also involved in some of the instore advertising platforms used by such shops, mainly focused on closed and continuous loop video shots that were transmitted across TV screens placed within the stores.

Like most great ideas, Benny's plan for Edgetech was very simple. He was able to describe the vision and the implementation to his audience without losing them on the way.

Benny's idea was to get the greatest leverage from his market position and draw out the technology of the network in order to build POS systems that were driven by a central server which could be customized down to the "nth" degree. In this way, a relatively small amount of hardware reengineering on the existing POS systems could accommodate a means of mass communication and content delivery that was dynamic and relevant. Within two years, Benny was confident that a large percentage of his clients would migrate their POS systems into a new, more dynamic format that could allow for personalization, and which would enable instore advertising to be married with the POS format. The great thing is that Benny has achieved and surpassed many of his targets.

His vision was based on a roll-out that covered all his existing sites within Hong Kong, and for those of us who were prepared to back him with venture capital, the real risk was execution-related. Benny already had a good relationship with his technology suppliers (Fujitsu, IBM, and Siemens) and we felt that the business could easily be scaled across the region.

When Benny first came to see us, his business plan relied to a certain degree upon a business partner who had indicated an interest in tying up with Benny in the form of a joint venture. This partner was interested in achieving a listing of his existing business, and both he and Benny felt that creating a partnership that was a partial owner of Edgetech would be beneficial for both of them.

While we at techpacific.com had some reservations, we were prepared to go along with the idea, especially since Benny was prepared to dilute his own equity interest in order to build the alliance. In short, at the outset, Benny would split his ownership of Edgetech into two parts; a direct ownership, and an indirect one that was a joint venture with his business associates.

techpacific.com made an offer to Benny that was based on this premise, and we signed the documents with a condition precedent that assumed he would close his deal with his associates, draw down on the venture capital, and move on with the implementation of his business plan.

Weeks passed, and then in late December we learned that Benny's business associate had become more demanding about his "cut" and was threatening to pull out of the deal if he didn't get a bigger share of the pie. This warning was based on the assumption that Benny was in a corner, and that if he didn't agree, then he was putting at risk some part of the capital that had been committed.

I was obviously concerned, since we had assumed that Benny had been able to complete his negotiations, and that his partner would be motivated to assist in the execution and roll-out of the plan due to their joint ownership of Edgetech. I called Benny, sometime between Christmas and New Year's Eve of 1999, and expressed my concern. I told him that we weren't worried about the fact that his partner wouldn't be a part of the deal from a financial standpoint, but that we *were* concerned that the product launch was somewhat dependent upon this part of the deal.

Benny was suitably concerned as well, but he assured me that all would be well, and that within two weeks, if his partner hadn't reconciled himself to the original arrangements, Benny would still go ahead, but with a different solution. Upon being pressed by me to share this solution, it turned out that Benny had put alternative arrangements in place almost six weeks earlier, and he was confident that Edgetech wouldn't be adversely affected due to any hiccups related to the product roll-out, or a more greedy partner.

As things turned out, Benny's original partner couldn't be reconciled, but he still moved ahead with alternative arrangements that included hiring a new CEO and spending more time in the business development area himself than originally planned. Edgetech is now well ahead of its game plan to be a regional player. One of the side benefits of implementing Benny's "alternative" plan is that the CEO who was eventually hired into the business has turned out to be much more dynamic than could have been expected, and has added breadth to the original business plan.

Benny was able to hope for the best, while also planning for the worst. He had hoped that his deal with his partner would work out, but he had also ensured that if there were problems, Edgetech could still continue on track.

6

Develop a Killer Instinct

It is our duty as men and women to proceed as though the limits of our abilities do not exist.

— Pierre Teilhard de Chardin

Knowing when to strike, and then being prepared to strike without compromise, is an essential tool for the technopreneur in Asia. Having the ability to strike beyond our usual range is the value that we gain from achieving a killer instinct.

The objective of the exercise, therefore, is to go beyond our self-imposed limits. In the rapid-fire Internet environment, delays caused by indecisiveness can lead to failure. Thus, developing a killer instinct is as important as developing the "killer app." (This term, which is widely used to mean a very successful business plan or application, was originally coined in the software industry to describe programs that have become entrenched in our everyday lives.)

When Chinadotcom was built on the foundations of the various components that were acquired by Peter Yip, no possibility for compromise was ever left on the table in the desire to achieve a public flotation.

The management team at Chinadotcom realized early on that in order to be a winner, they needed to be the first mover in the financial sense. This meant that Chinadotcom had to achieve a high degree of funding, and find a way to become listed on a major public market ahead of competitors that may well have been ahead in other areas.

The business may not have been the biggest in terms of traffic counts, and even to this day, Chinadotcom has more than its fair share of skeptics. However, the one thing that they have exhibited above all else is application of the killer instinct. Peter Yip, Peter Hamilton, Ian Henry (until his departure), and the investment banking groups at Lehman and Bear Stearns (including my colleague and partner, Johnny), were all part of the IPO team which exhibited a deep-seated determination that brooked no compromise.

In the Asia of tomorrow, as technology opportunities are created overnight, entrepreneurs will need to have a finely tuned sense of timing in order to survive. The companion to timing will be the killer instinct, which will ensure that survival can be turned into success.

The best example of how this characteristic will be needed in large measure can be seen in the likely surge in mergers and acquisitions (M&A) activity. Generic growth, even in the Internet world, won't be enough to fuel the kind of growth that is needed to be a winner. The alternative will be acquisitions and, in this field, striking with force and conviction cannot be substituted for, even by access to capital.

The entrepreneurs and businesses that succeed will do so due in part to their ability to build up a knowledge base of their competitors. Some of the leading Internet and technology businesses in Asia are investing large amounts of time and resources in looking at possible M&A targets and which are exercising their "killer instinct".

Delay and compromise often lead to failure in the Internet buyer's world, and when it comes to technology M&A, this will be brought into sharper focus. The short history of the Internet has already shown the power of such proactiveness, and deals such as Terra Networks' acquisition of Lycos, or the merger of AOL and Time Warner, are two of the more obvious examples of this quality at work.

The AOL/Time Warner deal, which was announced in early 2000, probably most typifies the extraordinary power of the Internet to affect traditional ways of thinking. The deal was prompted by a number of different forces coming together at the same time, and the opportunity for Steve Case at AOL to acquire a premium integrated platform was probably the most important determinant in the thought process from the point of view of AOL.

An article published in *Wired* magazine in September 2000 summed up this perspective in its lead editorial: "... our view, as often stated, is that pure online media companies leveraging a single platform will have a tough go of it. This is why Steve Case merged AOL with Time Warner, even when he was playing at the top of the online game ..."

This particular deal rewrote the operating rules that have governed the M&A business for Internet companies. Even though many Internet companies have traded to lower levels of valuation, the trend for consolidation or dramatic non-organic growth through mergers will continue for many years to come. As an interesting corollary, as many Internet companies fall in value, they are becoming more interesting to traditional companies that want to "kick-start" their expansion into the technology space.

For early-stage and young technology companies, alliances and mergers of interests with offline and traditional businesses are natural next steps following on from events such as the AOL/Time Warner merger. Founders, CEOs, and shareholders alike can draw inspiration and ask, "Why not us?" This would be a refreshing change from the usual caution that has characterized cross-industry marriages in the technology sector in the past.

I am particularly excited by this development as the newer areas of wireless communication and broadband access begin to take root here in Asia. We are already seeing some smaller and very innovative companies beginning to give up part of their equity to established companies in the "old" economy in order to accelerate their development, rather than have to rely solely on financial investors.

Within the Asian context, although such M&A activity isn't yet as prevalent as in the U.S. (although it will certainly become so as the markets mature and move on to the next phase of development), acquiring a killer instinct and being prepared to move quickly and with maximum force will be manifested in other ways. The new technology entrepreneur will have to act decisively when it comes to marketing arrangements and online alliances that can be tailored to maximum advantage.

In the past, strategic relationships often took a long time to become apparent. Two related parties might start negotiations after excruciating research and analysis, and after employing the use of a number of middlemen. In the "new" economy, this may not always be possible; in fact, middlemen are rarely likely to know more about the business than you, the entrepreneur. It's my view that the whole business environment is changing so rapidly that there are very few assumptions that hold true today which will still hold true in five years.

In this context, acting with force and speed in taking up opportunities that are presented will be a critical measure of success. It will be as important as managers' ability to sift through the research of their advisors. In fact, the past five years have shown that the successful technopreneur is one who has a well-developed instinct, and that it is the investors who have backed such people who have done well. The challenge, of course, is to find such people.

As a technopreneur, the challenge is to discover whether you are capable of such speed in action and can bed down your alliances and acquisitions to make them work.

An element of luck is also necessary. Most successful entrepreneurs will admit to the part that luck has played in their success, but I would say that luck can be manufactured, and that unless you actually create activity and take initiatives, you will never be in a position to find out if luck is on your side.

Exercises

Taekwondo

Go to the Web and search for the nearest place where you can go and learn the Korean martial art, taekwondo (TKD).

You will never find a better way of acquiring a killer instinct in a constructive environment. At techpacific.com, we have weekly TKD classes which help to create a great "bonding" environment, as well as keeping us physically fit. The rigid discipline of this martial art, combined with the team-oriented training courses, helps to build better partnerships. At the same time, you might find that you enjoy the physical exercise!

Learning from other winners' experiences

Get hold of a biography of J.P. Morgan. You won't find many entrepreneurs with a more developed killer instinct.

You might also want to read a recent book by Lisa Endlich entitled *Goldman Sachs — The Culture of Success*. It is a study of a modern-day organization that best resembles the "iron fist in a velvet glove" mentality. Anyone who has ever tried to compete with Goldman Sachs will know what I mean.

For a variation on the theme, you should also pick up one of the many biographies of the wartime exploits of Sir Winston Churchill. This great leader exhibited the killer instinct allied with the necessary determination to succeed.

> *Never give in, never give in, never, never, never, never, never ...*
>
> — *Sir Winston Churchill*

Sleepless in Seattle

If you really want to see what the killer instinct is all about, then decide to challenge Microsoft. Bill Gates and his band of merry brigands will teach you a thing or two about having a killer instinct.

There are many examples of Bill Gates's and Microsoft's killer instinct. However, the one that appeals to me most in this context is the way in which Microsoft Excel, the spreadsheet program, has now developed such a lead in the market that the original leader — Lotus 123 (does anyone still use this program?) — has been virtually eclipsed.

When I started my own career in 1984, I remember learning to use the Lotus package on my IBM PC. I also remember the very significant advantage that Lotus possessed due to their growing installed user base. For the next few years, new upgrades were produced that meant Lotus was able to stay ahead of the crowd. However, a

decade or so later it was almost as if I woke up one day and found that my Lotus 123 had morphed into Excel.

The real story here is probably the conquest of the world's personal computer industry by Microsoft, but I can assure you that the demise of Lotus 123 was planned and executed with the most compelling corporate killer instinct that you are ever likely to encounter.

Once upon a time...

In February 1999, techpacific.com got the chance to put its philosophy into action for the first time in a substantive way. This was the Bigsave.com deal, which we were asked to manage by one of our earliest shareholders, Jim Mellon. Jim is the founder and chairman of iRegent, an Isle of Man domiciled and Hong Kong listed investment management company.

The key turning point in the Bigsave.com deal, and an event that has highlighted for me the real power of the killer instinct, was the decision that needed to be taken by Bigsave with regard to Roldec Systems and their ownership of Roldec.com, a subsidiary and online seller of computers and computer peripherals.

I had just completed the initial due diligence in Huddersfield, England, where Roldec was headquartered. The management team, Denham Eke and Kazem Behjat, were both old friends of Jim, and were struggling to compete in the cut-throat world of selling discount computers against the likes of Dell.

Jim had seen the potential for migrating the business online, and adding it to his own nascent e-commerce idea (at that time still only a business plan), which was built around the URL www.bigsave.com.

It was clear to me, and to Jim, that the acquisition of Roldec.com and its core team, which was about to be made redundant, would be a great platform on which to build the Bigsave.com business.

The complication arose because it was equally obvious to us that Denham and Kazem could not really see the e-commerce angle of Bigsave.com, and wanted to save Roldec Systems. Their "price" for moving on into the future almost certainly meant the end of Roldec, which would have to call in the receivers if it couldn't attract the necessary working capital to stem the red ink.

Jim was capable of saving Roldec and probably still building Bigsave.com. However, the kindest thing to do would be to focus only on agreeing to acquire Roldec.com from the liquidator, and persuading Denham and Kazem to come and work at Bigsave.com and leave the past behind.

This emotional decision could have gone the wrong way, particularly since both of the key people were long-standing friends. Jim looked beyond the friendship and made the right decision. In this instance, the killer instinct was brought to bear, and the "right" decision was taken for the "right" reasons.

Raising the capital for Bigsave.com was the natural extension of the acquisition of Roldec Online, and it highlights how allowing the killer instinct to bring about the right decision is something that the Internet will force upon us with almost Darwinian inevitability. Within days of securing the Roldec Online business, Jim moved rapidly ahead with the fundraising part of the deal, and techpacific.com was retained to lead manage a process which was also our first significant transaction as a new company.

7

Do it — Now!

The universe favors the brave. When you resolve to lift your life to its highest level, the strength of your soul will guide you to a magical place with magnificent treasures.

— *Robin Sharma,*
The Monk Who Sold His Ferrari

A firm resolve, and the courage to act decisively and quickly, are essential ingredients in the makeup of a successful Internet or technology business leader. Acting with resolve and immediacy requires enormous reserves of bravery, but it's essential in the fast-moving world of the Internet. In my experience, timeframes not only get narrowed when implementing business plans, but the pace at which decisions are challenged by external events also increases exponentially in the "new" economy.

Building businesses in the Asian environment demands even quicker instincts and even more courage than in the U.S. or European markets. The whole of Asia seems to be racing to implement business models that were inspired "yesterday" and will be launched "tomorrow." The rush for capital, human resources, and technology support is intense, and running hard just to stand still is a common theme.

In fact, the wild swings in sentiment toward the Internet have only increased the pace at which businesses are being built. Since Asia was "late" to the Internet, there is some element of leapfrogging going on, and companies and entrepreneurs have to work within relatively tight timeframes in order to maintain their lead so that it's not taken by one of the new upstarts who are waiting just around the corner.

On a macro level, Asia is probably benefiting from its late start. The more painful adoption issues (2400 bps access speeds!) weren't an issue for some of the early businesses here in Asia as they were in the U.S., and many Internet companies have the luxury of working with newer technologies. I have read a number of reports from leading consultants and analysts that have taken the position that the market downturn of spring 2000 was much less acute in Asia due to this late entry. I would agree largely with this position. It's also apparent that the very large amounts of capital that have been raised by the venture capital and private equity industry have been virtually unscathed and remain uninvested. The message for would-be start-ups is therefore clear: get out there and raise hell!

The prerogative of the Internet is that immediacy counts for everything. Even when access speeds have reached the ultimate broadband Nirvana, the demand for "here and now" will drive people to new levels of innovation. This vision is now actively approaching reality, and the Internet experience is changing for a large part of the online population. Hand in hand with this change is an improvement in the overall availability of information that supports "e-biz" and allows companies to contemplate transactions across a much broader spectrum than just in advertising.

All of this means that for the foreseeable future, for the business person who competes in the Internet space in Asia, there is no such thing as tomorrow. Deadlines are always set as "today," and the only possible time for that new development was yesterday.

The ultimate test of this rule is still the implementation of the funding schedule. For all but the most well-connected businesses, securing the right amount of funding is a never-ending struggle in the early days of any business development. Resources have to be juggled so that business development is maintained at the same frenetic pace as in the race to secure funding.

It's not surprising, therefore, that the "first to market" advantage in Asia will continue to be linked to "first to finance," and this in itself will be linked to the founder's ability to sprint the marathon and stay ahead by running fast! Those of you who are runners will appreciate the counter-intuitive nature of this requirement. I know of many technopreneurs who are burnt-out even in the early stages of their own "race."

Doing it "now" also creates transparency of thought. This is an ingredient of success in all e-businesses, and shouldn't be a surprise to most experienced business people. Despite this, the benefits of immediacy and transparency are often a great surprise to new entrepreneurs. I have found this to be true in Asia regardless of whether the entrepreneur is young and still relatively inexperienced, or a seasoned professional who is ready to jump from the ship of corporate life into a new, independent existence. Transparency and immediacy help to fight this weakness.

Being transparent, and being able to act decisively, can be hampered by the fact that many of us are still hostage to our own experiences — that is, we carry a lot of baggage. This baggage might be cultural, and is often manifested in the way we try to react to situations by reference to what we believe to be the "correct" thing to do, rather than what we think is "right." This situation leads to inflexibility. I have found that those of us who strive to do the right thing are oftentimes confronted by people who assume that, because we are being unconventional, we are hiding something.

Times and attitudes are, of course, changing, and one of the great things about the technology revolution is that the pace of change is increasing. My advice is that if you are suffering from your own form of cultural baggage and are still sacrificing your flexibility by trying to conform, then you should regard this as a weakness and try to resolve it.

That's easier said than done, you might think, and I agree that change won't be easy. However, I believe that this weakness can only ultimately be addressed and resolved by people who have the necessary strength of character to move beyond what they *perceive* is correct, toward what is *actually* correct. At the end of the day, if you are more concerned about what other people, or the market in general, thinks about your idea, then you are less likely to be able to produce something that is truly revolutionary.

At techpacific.com we try to tackle these views head-on, and to educate people about the merits of immediacy and transparency. We try to help our partners understand that while caution has its merits, acting quickly in building momentum creates its own value. There are times when we may have suffered as a result of taking this attitude, but eventually our courage and conviction have won through.

Another common misconception (and, in fact, fear) in Asia is that if we adopt transparency in our business dealings, it may enable others to follow or copy our lead. These sorts of "conspiracy theories" are a pet hate of mine, and I continue to preach transparency wherever possible. For example, at techpacific.com, we are constantly being asked to sign non-disclosure agreements (NDAs). When we refuse to do so (it's our policy not to sign such agreements), we often have to spend an inordinate amount of time explaining why the business plan is safe with us and giving reassurance that we won't take undue advantage of the concept.

We understand and appreciate, of course, the value of intellectual property. Our refusal to sign NDAs has more to do with the huge volume of deals that we have to handle, which makes signing such agreements impossible. At the same time, however, it's interesting to see how different people react to our position.

Since June 1999, when we first established the M^3 program, we have "lost" only two deals, out of the thousands that we have processed, as a result of entrepreneurs not wanting to go forward without a signed NDA. On both of those occasions, the entrepreneur was too impatient to take the time to consider our view.

In every other case, once we explained our position, the people with whom we were dealing felt very comfortable and the deal review process continued. It's my opinion that this overwhelming acceptance of our position is due to our transparent methods, where we make clear to the market our modus operandi and help our partners to track the progress of their deal through the review process.

For the successful new entrepreneur, having established the value of momentum (consider the whole concept of "first mover advantage," which is all about momentum), we then help them to understand how this is connected with transparency of thought and action. It's the rare business person who isn't inspired by the Yahoos and Amazons of this world, or, in Asia, by companies such as Sina.com and Netease, which have built upon their position of leadership and the first mover advantage that was created in the early part of their commercial existence.

In Asia, very few businesses or start-ups can truly claim the first mover space. However, companies such as Chinadotcom, Infosys, Sina.com, and techpacific.com are examples of how the momentum of being an early or first mover can be transformed into commercial success. These companies have used their first mover position to create awareness and clarity regarding their business. The market understands what they do and how they do it. After all, what's the point of being first, or of being quick to discern a market, if the market doesn't understand your position?

"Doing it now" is a value that lies very close to the surface in the "new" economy. This is obvious when we look at the way in which first movers in their markets have built a position of leadership which can only be sustained by continued adherence to the philosophy that prompt action is imperative.

The Internet forces immediacy, not just on people and communities, but on regions and governments as well. A great example of this confluence of circumstance, where the Internet has collided with a massive change in economic opportunity and developmental need, is China. For many Western financiers and business people, China has long represented a "holy grail" where the billion or so consumers need to be provided with products and services that might be supplied by the West.

The Internet is probably the single biggest force of change that is being played out in this vast country, and the leapfrogging of technology (China is already the leader in a variety of areas, such as mobile phone users and cabled homes) means that China will drive innovation as much as use technology.

While the authorities have attempted, at times, to contain the spread of information that the Internet makes possible, they have also benefited from the fact that Chinese entrepreneurs and technological prowess have created one of the deepest pools of talent on the planet. In fact, Chinese technology business people possess some of the most extreme qualities of "do it now-ism" in Asia, and as a result are creating some of the biggest and most spectacular winners around. By this I mean that an essential quality of many of China's technology and Internet entrepreneurs is their desire to move decisively and quickly. These qualities are standing them in good stead, and are helping them to overcome obstacles not encountered in more open and advanced economies.

In many ways, therefore, China is one of the best examples of how the spirit of "do it now" can transform ideas into reality.

Action will remove the doubt that theory cannot solve.
— Tehyi Hsieh

Immediacy and transparency go hand in hand with courage and decisiveness. It's only by "doing" that business empires can be built.

I would like to conclude this part of the chapter with a contribution from my colleague and friend Ali Siddiqui, who, at just twenty-four, is already a serial entrepreneur. He is also one of the most self-assured and yet humble people in this whole Internet space in Asia. Apart from being a very valued member of our team and a founder employee (along with Kenyon Lee, Shahzad Ashfaque, Joey Borromeo, and Yuda Udomritthruj), Ali is also a founder of PlanetArabia.com (www.planetarabia.com). His experience of building that business is a wonderful example of how "do it — now!" can work in the real world.

Do it — now!

Ali Siddiqui, co-founder of PlanetArabia.com

How we got involved in the whole process of thinking about building a leading portal and destination site for the Arab world was very straightforward. I was still a student at Cornell University at the time (late 1998), as were my colleagues and co-founders, and the whole Internet market was in the early stages of its tremendous growth.

We had been following the development of Starmedia, El Sitio, and the other companies in the Latin Internet space, and one day we were discussing how the Arab Internet space was still very early in its development. It was so early, in fact, that when we wanted to find Arab websites ourselves, there were very few to choose from.

There were obviously huge gaps in the market, and therefore many opportunities in this space, so we went ahead and started building a website. The idea was to build a community where our friends could spend time and meet other people. Building a business was a vague part of our intentions, but since none of us had yet graduated, the initial push was really to try and create something neat and cool, rather than make a formal business out of it.

Our first steps in building the site took place in January 1999. By May, after working in the evenings and on weekends, we had our first beta running and we then incorporated the company. In early June, we began to negotiate with partners such as Reuters. It was only at that point that we realized we didn't have any business cards! (We concluded many of our early partnerships before we got around to having business cards printed.) We became aware of how focused we had been on building a product and how we had neglected many other important items, such as a business plan.

Thus far, we had just US$19,000 in capital and a business plan was necessary to raise funds. We wrote one in June 1999 — it was just eight pages long.

Just as the Latin American Internet space exploded from 1998 onwards, the Arab Internet space is exploding now. Since we launched PlanetArabia, there have been many horizontal and vertical websites launched that target the Arab market. We were three young guys with little experience and limited resources. Looking back, the one thing that we had going for us was that we made it to market early, and we were convinced that we had to "do it — now!"

The fact that we made it to market early and didn't deliberate much before going ahead is the primary reason for our leadership position. Some of this was luck — we were at college with few responsibilities and had the time to build PlanetArabia. But most of it was a combination of determination and speed. After initially deciding on the concept, the team spent very little time thinking about it. We just kept working until we launched. Of course, we made some mistakes — when we look back now we're horrified at our ignorance — but our momentum carried us through.

PlanetArabia was conceived at the Cornell University campus in January 1999 and went live the following September. Five months after going live, it was ranked the number one Arab portal by *Internet Al-Arab* magazine. PlanetArabia has won a number of awards and is a leading online network for the Arab world. We were able to attract incubation capital from techpacific.com early in our business life, and this is one of the key "lucky breaks" that arose from our ability to "do it — now".

I would encourage all aspiring entrepreneurs to be focused and brave enough to back their convictions. There is no substitute for hard work, and we all need lucky breaks, but our experience has taught us the value of speed and decisiveness.

Exercises

Yes!

If you have a great idea, and you think you deserve to be funded, then go to www.techpacific.com and fill in the application form for entrepreneurs. Do it now!

Our whole business operation is geared around being responsive to people who are brave enough to take up the challenge, and this exercise will test your ability to communicate your dreams. If nothing else, the act of having to explain your idea to a group of talented people who scrutinize business plans for a living will do you more good than harm.

Be warned though as less than 1% of all applicants get funded, so you may not be successful.

Seizing the day

Our chairman, Robert Owen, seems to spend all his time compiling lists and then ticking off the things listed. His lists usually consist of things he needs to do in the very short term.

In this exercise, take a piece of paper and list three things you want to do at some stage (not in the short term) in your personal life. Be specific. An objective such as "be the best that I can be" is too vague for the purposes of this exercise (however noble it might be). Try to be at least reasonably realistic. For example, my list of objectives might include:

- Run a marathon.
- Catch a 1000-pound black marlin.
- Take my wife to the south of France on holiday next spring.

Over the next two days, reduce the list to the *one thing* that is most compelling — and then do it.

That's right, just do it.

Now, on another piece of paper, write down three things you would like to do in your professional life. Be realistic about any timeframes.

In my case, these might be:

- Hire a head of human resources to help Robert and Johnny take control of our business.
- Make sure our Intranet site is online within three months.
- Finish writing this book.

Again, over the next couple of days, whittle the three objectives down to one — and then, just do it.

Once upon a time...

One of my favorite "do it — now!" stories relates to the events that led to our investment in Netease, the highly successful Chinese portal created in 1995 by William Ding.

In May 1999, a few months into our life as a start-up, and before we had managed to build our team, Johnny called me about an opportunity to help Netease gain some breathing space by arranging an early stage investment in the business by techpacific.com.

With Netease, William Ding originated Chinese-language email. The development of Netease into a leading portal site in the Chinese language was built upon an unmatched local network that provides Internet users with local news and content. This approach led to a massive ramp-up in subscribers, and Netease is now one of the most visited websites not only in China, but in Asia.

It is William's belief and conviction that his company will become a global leader in terms of traffic and visitors over the next decade, and I would certainly go along with this view. (I should disclose at this point that, in addition to techpacific.com's investment in Netease, I am also a very small personal shareholder in Netease, which is a NASDAQ listed company.)

The real challenge in May 1999, when we were presented with the opportunity, was that while we didn't doubt the huge potential of the business and were totally committed to the Netease team, structuring the deal and enabling it to go ahead was going to be difficult, to say the least. The capital was needed urgently, as the competition was at our heels, but our ability to invest in the company was opaque in legal terms, given the regulatory environment in China that was still being developed.

In the final analysis, there was no single solution that seemed safe or prudent. The only way to proceed was to take the kind of risk with the structure that wouldn't have been acceptable to most traditional venture capitalists, and which would mean placing faith in William as an individual.

Johnny (who was handling the discussion with Netease), Robert Owen, and I debated the matter for a week. We had two critical decisions to make:

1. Should we go with a structure that had inherent risk (a risk that we couldn't really take out of the deal)?
2. Should we commit capital that the firm didn't possess, and therefore provide personal guarantees in order to close the deal?

I was in New Zealand on the day that we finally took a deep breath and decided that we had to back our instincts. We were of one mind that our total comfort with the business in terms of its dynamics would be enough to overcome the problems that were inevitable with the structure. We decided that we would willingly take the risk ourselves, and we were confident that our outside shareholders would also be willing to take the risk if they were presented with the opportunity. We knew that we couldn't dot all the Is and cross all the Ts in the usual way, but our instincts told us to go ahead anyway and just do it — and do it now!

Robert, Johnny, and I provided 25% of the capital needed to do the deal, with techpacific.com stumping up 25% and our shareholders providing the rest.

Netease has turned out to be a key relationship. It has enabled us to build a China business of a depth and breadth that otherwise wouldn't have been possible.

The investment itself has been rather profitable as well. Since we initiated that transaction, techpacific.com has raised further finance on two occasions as the regulatory environment has become clearer, bringing in investors such as Goldman Sachs, Softbank, and News Corp.

Johnny reminded me during the writing of this book that "do it — now!" also requires an ability to change one's mind about a process or a solution if circumstances change. Quite often, when we agree to forge ahead, we do it in the knowledge that our determination may need to be tempered at some stage. Such a change of mind isn't a sign of weakness, but of strength.

This doesn't mean that we should be in any way lax in our commitment; rather, it means that we need to back up our courage with the willingness to reconsider whether the way we are doing something is the best or fastest way to get us to our destination.

Perhaps W. Somerset Maugham put it best when he wrote:

> *Like all weak men, he laid an exaggerated stress on not changing one's mind.*

8

Long Live Beta!

Always make new mistakes!!

— *Esther Dyson,*
Release 2.0: A Design for Living in the Digital Age

In Guy Kawasaki's remarkable book *Rules for Revolutionaries*, he urges people to be prepared to be "crappy" and to launch their product or service even though it may not appear to be 100% ready. It's often more important, he says, to be first to market. His advice is based on his long years in Silicon Valley and his experiences at Apple Computer, where "insanely great products" would never have come to life if they hadn't been launched despite having a whole series of "imperfections."

Many of the books that have dealt with the history of Apple Computer have noted the early problems with the Macintosh. It had too little memory, no external floppy drive, a propensity to crash, a premium price, and so on. But the attractions of this cool new user-friendly personal computer were enough to override its many faults, and the launch proved to be one of the most successful product launches in the history of computing.

Apart from Apple Computer, of course, there is a long list of product launches that weren't "ready" but which turned into winners. I remember reading about the first generation of Mosaic (the Web browser), where the underlying problems were greater than the apparent advantages but where the launch allowed people to glimpse the future.

There is no point in waiting for perfection, because there is no such thing as a perfect product. Even if something *appears* to be ready, it's in our nature to keep tinkering with it. How often have you woken up and started re-tooling something that appeared to be ready the night before? The whole idea of "sleeping on it" stems from our inclination for review and reconsideration.

There is always some amendment that could be made. And this is where the beta version of a website or enabling software comes into its own. The Asian technopreneur will learn early on that the world waits for no one, and that having a beta site works wonders that won't be appreciated until after the event.

In fact, most of the early successes have proved that waiting for clarity or for a better site isn't an option. Go and ask the guys at Acer, in Taiwan, if the first PC they

ever shipped was perfectly ready. Go to LG, in Korea, and ask to be shown the first MP3 device, and compare it with the current offering.

For that matter, if you were to ask Peter Hamilton (COO at Chinadotcom) what he now thinks of the early version of their website, I'm sure he would be able to identify a litany of deficiencies that are obvious to him in retrospect. The fact is that the site was launched. Regular upgrades since then have incorporated new features and minor revisions to keep it dynamic.

The quotation that opens this chapter is from Esther Dyson, who uses it in her signature file. She makes the point very elegantly in her book *Release 2.0: A Design for Living in the Digital Age* that we shouldn't avoid making mistakes, but should learn from them.

> *I still have new mistakes to make. The challenge is not to avoid mistakes, but to learn from them. And then go forward and make new ones and learn again. There's no shame in making new mistakes if you acknowledge them and benefit from them.*

Got the message? If you have your own version of an insanely great idea or product, bust your balls to get the idea to market, and as long as it works, and as long as it takes the service or function offered to a new level, you won't need to worry about the imperfections until the next version, by which time you will have created a market.

Sure, some people might complain, but great products will be recognized as such, and the doubters and the naysayers will only help you to get a better version of the product into the market next time around.

Go ahead, have fun, and, in the words of Guy Kawasaki, be "crappy." Remember Hubert Humphrey's advice:

> *More progress results from the violent execution of an imperfect plan than the perfection of a plan to violently execute.*

Exercises

Metamorphosis

Adopt a caterpillar and watch it become a butterfly.

Seriously, things change and all products need a beginning. By appreciating how things "morph," you will become a better technopreneur.

Absorb this poem

William Bennett, who wrote *The Children's Book of Virtues*, composed this wonderful poem:

The Man who misses all the fun
Is he who says "it can't be done."
In solemn pride he stands aloof
And greets each venture with reproof.
Had he the power he'd efface
The history of the human race;
We'd have no radio or motor cars,
No streets lit by electric stars;
Neither telegraph nor telephone,
We'd linger in the age of stone.
The world would sleep if things were run
By men who say "it can't be done."

The poem says a lot about those people who will sit on the sidelines and tell you you're not ready. Never be afraid to get your ideas off the ground.

This is my favourite quote in the book.

Kick butt!

Go to www.kickbutt.com and order Guy Kawasaki's book. It's a great tool to have by your side when you take that first step into entrepreneurship.

Once upon a time...

Having a beta is all about having ideas. Without an initial idea, you can't really get to first base, and without getting to first base, you can never score the run. In fact, having a beta is actually all about acting on your idea, and then refining it as you learn more about the practical application in the real world.

> *The best way to have an idea is to have lots of ideas.*
> *— Linus Pauling*

It wouldn't have been possible to set up techpacific.com without first making the decision to launch the business when we weren't even a real company. The URL that we acquired was in the name of one of my colleagues, Ali

Siddiqui, who at the time was studying at Cornell University. We managed to obtain our first working assignment when we didn't even have a corporate identity. I remember typing up the mandate letter using good old font manipulation on Word for Macintosh, and hoping it would come out looking official.

That assignment led to the company's first couple of months' expenses being substantially paid for; it also provided us with the ability to start building our team.

Launching techpacific.com on the basis of a raw idea was our own version of "long live beta," and it has taught us the value of being prepared to stake a claim in the space in which we wanted to operate.

It also taught us the power of the market, and how years of preparation could never take the place of the experience that we have accumulated through actually doing business, rather than just talking about doing business.

Being prepared to start running when you can barely walk embodies many of the ideas described in this book, and is very relevant to what is happening in Asia today. If you are a talented entrepreneur, and regardless of whether you are stuck in a large corporation or are fresh out of college, putting your toe in the water is the key first step that will help to define everything else.

When we first started techpacific.com, we knew the value of the beta test and were prepared to extend it to the launch of our website. We completed the first cut of the site and launched the interactive M[3] program at the end of June 1999 when most of our friends thought our site was nothing more than overblown brochure-ware. There are probably people out there who *still* think our site is overblown brochure-ware! But in the first few weeks after launch, when we started to attract online applications from entrepreneurs and from investors who wanted to join our program, we knew we had a winner on our hands.

I read Esther Dyson's book soon after our initial launch in August 1999. Although I was already familiar with many of the points she makes in the book, the message came through more powerfully now that I was involved in running my own business and was directly accountable for my actions. The experience of launching our own beta site into a live market gave me the feeling (sometimes called literary vertigo) that her words had been written specifically with me and techpacific.com in mind.

I have also been involved with another group of talented entrepreneurs at a technology company in Hong Kong named Entone. With all due respect to the many other deals in which we have invested our resources, I consider Entone to be one of my favorite experiences thus far — which is saying something when I consider some of the truly great businesses and people that I have had the good fortune to be associated with. Companies such as gogo.com, webmedia, Netease, Gorilla Communications, eWarna, and UBQT (which is also a name worth remembering) are on their own way to fame and fortune, but Entone stands out even among this crowd. (Again, a point of disclosure: I am a member of the board of directors of Entone.)

Mark Evensen and Tim Warren, the two founders of Entone, worked together at Hong Kong Telecom as software engineers in the late 1990s. Their vision was based on building a product that allows rich content to be accessed on an efficient and fast basis by traditional digital subscriber line (DSL) networks (a common and increasingly popular infrastructure solution by telcos for the "last mile" connectivity problem).

While they were in the process of creating their core product offering for this application, Mark and Tim also got into a number of exciting projects, including teaming up with a leading Hong Kong manufacturing company, V-tech, which is well known for its manufacture of cordless phones, children's computer games, and set-top boxes.

Entone was started by Mark and Tim on the back of their own contacts in the Asian market. With no capital to fall back on, they built their company "brick by brick," resorting to selling their consulting expertise in order to gain revenue and buy time to create their software product.

I first became involved with Entone in late October 1999, and since then I have come to admire the way in which Entone has used beta testing and beta products to forge ahead with their business plan. Entone is unique in its space, and is certainly one of only a handful of companies in Asia that can be described as being "pure tech."

For Entone, building and working with a beta product has been so necessary that they probably don't understand what all the fuss is about when I highlight this aspect of their development. Entone is a powerful role model that can help other entrepreneurs to appreciate the power of utilizing beta products.

Since setting up Entone in early January 1999, Mark and Tim have created substantial shareholder value by pursuing their convictions. They have done so in an environment that has traditionally been devoid of true technology R&D on a commercial basis. (That's because many companies and entrepreneurs who are very R&D-focused migrate to the United States to develop their companies.) In order to create the right formula, Entone burned the candle at both ends, and when they needed to convince people that they had more than just a concept that could accelerate packet switching and content delivery across DSL networks, they reverted to using beta products and effectively created their product from the ground up.

I was part of this process when I became a director of Entone. I don't profess to understand the whole technology behind the product development, but I *can* attest to the vast strides the company has made by way of beta testing and beta products. Entone embodies the principles set out in Esther Dyson's book.

A word of warning: don't be tempted to settle for a less-than-ready business plan or product if all you are doing is being lazy. Be focused on quality, make sure that you can gather the best team around you, and never lose sight of what made you start in the first place. But once you have those things in your grasp — go for it. Go for it!

9

Network, Network, Network

The usefulness or utility of a network equals the square of the number of its users.

— *Metcalfe's Law*

The well-heeled MBA graduate of Stanford, Harvard, or MIT will likely tell you that the academic content of their degree has proved to be of less value to them than the networking they did during their MBA program.

In these early days of the Internet, Asia is like a village. This is unlikely to change in the near future (one only has to look across to the United States to realize that this is still true even in the world's largest marketplace), and this revolution, like all others before it, has a core set of trailblazers who are worth knowing.

Radiating out from this core, like the rays of the sun, are the network enablers who are also worth knowing in order to be able to build the alliances and friendships that will count toward ultimate success.

Asians have long known the value of networking. The cocktail and dinner party circuits of most Asian cities, from Seoul to Bangkok and beyond, have resonated with the purr of satisfied supplicants who have drawn out their journey in order to "connect" with the best. The Internet takes this process, purges it of elitism (networking is no longer about cocktail parties and tennis clubs), and adds to it a concentration that is unique and unparalleled.

For you to even contemplate success, you will need to get your product known. Networking allows entry to the vital first step.

Networking requires discipline and consistency. One of the most successful proponents of this skill is my partner,

Johnny, whose God-given charisma and good nature have enabled him to build a network of contacts in the "e-biz" world in Asia that is truly second to none.

It's no exaggeration to say that a large part of our early success at techpacific.com is due to the help and support we have derived from our network.

The new media, a core element of which is the Internet, liberate the individual and allow the power of the network to be leveraged by all. The effect of this new paradigm was brought home to me when I read this piece written by Paul Kennedy in his 1993 book, *Preparing for the 21st Century*. He wrote:

> *Fifty or sixty years ago, radio and television were beginning to make their impact, but only among a relatively few rich societies; as our century closes, they are affecting peoples — especially younger generations — across the globe. Moreover, whilst it once appeared that the new media would enhance the power of the governments (as for example Orwell argued in* 1984*), their effect recently has been the opposite: breaking the state monopolies of information, permeating national boundaries, allowing peoples to hear and see how others do things differently.*

The next part of the paragraph is the key:

It has also made richer and poorer countries more aware of the gap between them than was possible a half century ago, and stimulated legal and illegal migration.

Although Kennedy's point is somewhat different, it reminds me of the enormous changes now made possible because of the information revolution. It also highlights the power of a personal network when people all have access to the same source of ready information.

The great thing about networks is that they can build upon themselves. Anyone who has built any kind of Net business is living testimony to this tenet, and one of the

most successful networks of the Internet age is surely Kleiner Perkins Caufield & Byers (www.kpcb.com). Kleiner Perkins is one of the great venture capital companies of Silicon Valley, and the inventor of the whole concept of networks among commonly owned enterprises within the technology sphere. Established in 1972, and based in Menlo Park, California, they have been investors in, and influential thinkers behind, such great successes as @HomeNetwork, Amazon, Genentech, and Sun Microsystems, to name just a few. This *keiretsu* (Kleiner Perkins's own description, borrowed from the Japanese) has seen the creation of huge winners among their investee companies.

It is my view that the Asian experience will prove that the impact of networking will be even more acute over the next decade. By investing capital in corporations and start-up companies, Kleiner establishes only the first link in a chain of value creation that leverages the collective knowledge of the partnership. Partners and senior executives of the firm make it a priority to leverage their personal and collective networks in order to enhance the success of their investee and portfolio companies, and in this way they diminish the risk of failure.

I would recommend that you take a few minutes to visit their website and read about the *keiretsu* approach taken by this truly great organization which continues to inspire me personally despite my generally deep-seated skepticism for traditional venture capital firms.

In an Asian context, the power of networking for the new entrepreneur can be established by reference to that wonderful organization IandI (www.iandiasia.com), which was established by my colleague and friend, Jonathan Hakim. IandI stands for "Internet and Information." The organization was set up as a means of communication and networking among professionals involved in the Internet in Hong Kong.

Network, network, network

Jonathan Hakim, founder of iandiAsia, Boom.com, and Gorillasia.com

It is my opinion that networking is generally undervalued by start-ups on the Internet, especially here in Asia.

At IandI we see people join the events when they are first trying to break into the market. Later, however, they attend much less often, and start to feel that they have too much work to do to justify going out and "socializing."

My own view is that if they were to dedicate a certain amount of time each week to getting out and "socializing," or networking, with other people in their space, new opportunities and discussions would arise that might make the work they are so caught up in easier and in some cases unnecessary.

I would like to remind those people who think they don't have enough time to get out to IandI events that networking is like exercising. It takes some extra energy to do it, and the rewards aren't always immediately apparent, so people make excuses not to do it. But if they would take the time to attend, it would make a lot of their day-to-day work easier by opening up new opportunities.

One of the most obvious obstacles is that it's really easy to get discouraged about networking. You may attend and enjoy an IandI event, but by the next morning you can't see how the people you met the night before will be immediately helpful. This may stop you from going along the next time when you have the excuse of a lot of work to do. However, this may be just the night when you could meet someone who could lead you to someone else with a good opportunity for you.

Real networking isn't about how much the other people can help you. It's about how much you can help other people. I believe that the more people you help, the more people will help you. So, even if you feel you are God's gift to the Internet, you should still get out there and help other people. The more you help others in the industry, the better the industry gets and the more opportunities it opens up for everyone — yourself included.

This is the motivating force behind IandI — to nurture the Internet industry in Asia. It may be a little egotistical of me, but I honestly believe that this feeling of helping others, sharing information, and being open has spread throughout IandI and has helped a lot of people who used to be very protective and ungiving to open up. A lot of the people I have had speak at IandI events used to be from the wrong side of the camp — they were the ones who made it difficult for the little guys to get any business done. But when they come and speak at IandI, I can see them catch the feeling there and I hope that it makes them a little more open to helping others.

I would encourage readers of this book to visit the organization's website at www.iandiasia.com in order to experience the breadth and reach of this strictly not-for-profit network.

There are now IandI hubs in Singapore, Shanghai, Beijing, Bangkok, Taipei, and San Francisco. In the original home base of Hong Kong, the weekly meetings have become the core of Hong Kong's Internet and Web society. The gatherings, held at the Furama Hotel, routinely attract hundreds of people.

Networking isn't just about going to meetings, however. There are dozens of examples of how valuable networking has become in this "new" economy, when knowing the right people isn't a matter of nepotism, but a transparent means of achieving an objective by way of sharing common interests.

In fact, the whole of the Internet is really about the power of the network. If people have difficulty understanding that concept, then they might as well not be involved in businesses that depend on the Internet.

Exercises

Read *Release 2.0*

Read Esther Dyson's book *Release 2.0: A Design for Living in the Digital Age*. If you don't read the whole book, at least read the introduction.

> *The net is not a global village but an environment in which a profusion of different villages will flourish.*
>
> — *Esther Dyson,* Release 2.0

Using your Rolodex

Open your Rolodex, or your card box, and place the cards in front of you.

Take a piece of paper and write your name in the centre. Then write down the names from all the cards in random order. When you've done that, add the names of people you know but whose card you don't have. Try to fill the page.

When you have finished listing the names, take a marker pen and start connecting the names of people who you know are acquainted with each other. For example, your page may include the names

Ian K
Jim B
Claire F
Lesley Z
Allan W
Frank Q
Guy K
Ilyas K

By the time you are finished, you'll find that the names comprise a network with you in the middle. They are all connected through you, though they may also be connected in other more direct ways. For example, Ian K was in the same firm as Lesley Z. Lesley Z used to work for Claire F, who is also a neighbor of Guy K. Allan W was at school with Frank Q, and Frank Q's brother is the lawyer who represents Ilyas K.

Get the picture?

Now use your network to your advantage.

IandI / Wired Island

When you are next in Singapore, Taiwan, Hong Kong, or Thailand, attend the local IandI meeting. If you feel inspired to start your own chapter in a city that hasn't yet benefited from IandI, contact me and I will put you in touch with the key organizers. IandI is a great way to get networked and, ultimately, to get noticed.

Visit the website of Wired Island (www.wiredisland.com), which is based in Singapore and is a commercial site founded on similar principles to IandI.

Once upon a time ...

At techpacific.com, we not only understand the power of the network, but we use it to our advantage in a direct way that continues to surprise us with the power and the advantage it has bestowed upon our business.

In late August 1999, we decided to try and complete a second round of fundraising. This round (which was actually our Series "A") was completed with Softbank as lead manager, and although the total amount raised was very modest, we decided to reserve about US$1 million worth of equity for what is commonly known as a "friends and family" round. In this way, we were able to distribute small packages of shares to friends and supporters who wished to invest in techpacific.com, and who we knew would not only be helpful as we grew, but who represented a powerful network in their own right.

We ended up with about forty extra people as shareholders from across Asia, Europe, and the United States, ranging from those who invested as little as $5,000 in shares to those investing $50,000 and more. These people include professionals from all walks of life and experience.

Since the time of that distribution, the support that we have gained from this network of investment bankers, venture capitalists, analysts, and corporate leaders has been far greater than just the amount of money they invested. In many ways, in fact, the value created by having people with an alignment of interest is so much greater than the value of the shares they hold that we have to try hard not to feel embarrassed by the insignificance of the value of their shares in techpacific.com compared to their overall wealth.

The effect, however, of having someone who is both a friend and a shareholder look out for our interests as a small company has been invaluable. To those of you in our network who are reading this book, thanks!

The newly minted technopreneur would be wise to follow our example and build networks of contacts based on a common interest. It's not an easy thing to do, and you have to be able to distinguish between those people who don't want or need an economic interest in order to be helpful, and those who are happy to become financially involved.

The best type of network contact occurs when your company really doesn't need capital and you can build alliances through acquaintanceship or common interests. In our case, we could have raised the amount of dollars many times over with capital from serious institutions, but we wanted our network to be really meaningful to those involved in it, and so we went out of our way to create this valuable franchise of smaller shareholders.

Since the initial fundraising, techpacific.com has raised funds on a couple more occasions, and each time we have been focused on ensuring that we enhance our network as well as raising capital. This meant that we added a few more individual investors to each round of fundraising in addition to the institutional and corporate shareholders that were solicited. These steps have proven useful and I can say that, in our case, Metcalfe's Law has proven to be true. We took great care to ensure that whilst we were a privately held corporation, we produced regular newsletters that could be distributed to our shareholders in order to keep them in touch with our development. Since we became a public company in April 2000, our shareholders have become much more varied and diverse, and the whole concept of networking via our shareholders has taken on a new form. However, for many readers of this book, the advantages of distributing shares in your company to people who can be helpful when you are still private is a powerful lesson in the benefits of a network.

A word of warning: in many countries, there are rules and regulations governing the distribution of stock, even in a private company. If you are going to sell or distribute stock to people other than your staff and family or friends, then make sure that you get the correct and appropriate legal advice. This will ensure that you don't cross the line, either by making what constitutes an "offer" to the public (there are rules against this in most countries), or by selling securities in a manner that conflicts with securities regulations.

Another powerful example of the importance of networking can be found in Gorilla Asia (www.gorillasia.com). Gorilla was founded by Jonathan Hakim, who runs our incubation program (tplabs) at techpacific.com. Jonathan is a serial entrepreneur. He was also one of the founders of the highly successful IandI and of Boom, Asia's first online brokerage firm.

Gorilla is all about the Internet professional, and has established a unique presence through bringing together a wonderfully diverse and stimulating range of people and firms involved in the Internet. Gorilla organizes conferences and seminars that are involved with the whole technology theme, while at the same time running a website that has become the destination of choice for Internet professionals in Asia, but focusing at this stage on Greater China.

In building and maintaining this eco-system, Gorilla has created and leveraged its own unique network, and their bulletin boards and forums are routinely buzzing with informative sessions that are relevant across the industry. Gorilla is run by a truly innovative bunch of people, headed by Trevor Richter. It has grown since its inception to become one of the most active formal networks connecting Internet professionals, including the most switched-on investment analysts and leaders of Internet businesses, in the Greater China area.

In a recent thread about e-tailing, equity analysts covering the Internet from CSFB and other investment banks were joined by incubator managers, e-tail and e-commerce company executives, venture capital investors, and regular Internet professionals in a debate that was conducted at such high levels of quality and informed opinion that it was better than many consulting papers.

Given that Jonathan has often been described as one of the most networked guys in Asia, it's not surprising that Gorilla Asia has become such a successful business (disclosure point: techpacific.com owns around 25% of Gorilla Asia). But even aside from its business aspects, it's a stunning example of what networking is all about.

10

Free the Mind

Nirvana is not somewhere else; it resides in your own mind. Reach out and possess it, since it belongs to you anyway.

— Anonymous

The successful technopreneur in Asia will have to be able to think laterally and free his or her mind to the fullest and most extreme extent.

Who says you need to follow any rules, anyway?

In building businesses on the Web in Asia, free association will work better than any blind devotion to models of success that work elsewhere.

There is no lack of books extolling the virtues of applying U.S. business models to businesses in Asia. But the real winners in Asia will be those who are imaginative and creative enough to dispense with those models and develop new, Asia-specific approaches to business decision-making in their place.

Lateral thinking brings its own rewards. Those of your colleagues who think outside the box are the ones most likely to have a real impact on your success, but only if your own mind is open. Think about it. How likely are you to benefit from innovation within your organization if you aren't open to new ideas?

In creating techpacific.com, Johnny and I broke many of the rules that we had come to value in our former lives as investment bankers. We spoke our mind to all comers; and we didn't just shed our suits when we came to our new offices, we shed our inhibitions.

Our way of doing business has attracted some controversy. However, it's usually the "dinosaurs," the "old" economy types, who are most vocal in their criticism. My policy on those occasions when our approach has been questioned has been to ignore the naysayers and to focus on what I believe are the essential ingredients of success. By and large, most of our critics have either disappeared or changed their opinions anyway!

I believe that this approach has enabled techpacific.com to create and sustain a valuable business, and along the way I have had the pleasure of helping entrepreneurs to build some wonderful companies in their own right. As you recall, one of my greatest pleasures is that we have been able to raise capital for some great entrepreneurs.

Learning to think laterally enables winners to create their

own set of rules. In the process, they inspire others who look to them for leadership.

One of the dangers of success is a reluctance to move away from a proven formula, so while the results of lateral thinking can be powerful in the early days, it's not always easy to sustain the ability to continue being innovative. Even in smaller companies, early-stage employees sometimes feel that they "own" the "rights" to the way in which their companies are managed. Many books have been written about how to nurture free thinking within large corporations — and it is paradoxical but true that this same danger exists in virtually all stages of development. So, for the Asian technopreneur, "free the mind" needs to be a constant and ever-present refrain.

Freeing the mind requires honesty and sincerity of purpose. A by-product of this, and an important value in itself, is the good that will be done to your heart and your mind by the freedom that you create.

Go to your bosom:
Knock there, and ask your heart what it doth know.
— *William Shakespeare,* Measure for Measure

I firmly believe that freedom is a quality that breeds success. The final objective of any business is to achieve success, and so the final objective of this book is to encourage you to free your mind of any prejudices that might be holding you back.

Let me share something with you that is essential to techpacific.com, and which I believe is relevant to young entrepreneurs across Asia. When we started, we decided that we would treat entrepreneurs with a degree of respect and dignity that was sadly lacking in Asia. We felt that capital providers and investors in Asia tended to treat entrepreneurs in such a way that the value of their ideas was diminished by the procedure that the entrepreneur had to follow just to get a decent audience, never mind getting funded.

As most of my readers will no doubt know, obtaining capital in Asia was often more a case of *who* you knew, rather than *what* you knew. By operating from a mind-set where we treated entrepreneurs as our equals, we broke some rules, and the only way we could sustain this approach was by freeing our minds.

Today, with a brand that is recognized across Asia and a company that is publicly listed, when I am asked why we have managed to grow in an environment that has been largely geared toward backing the next "fashion," I highlight this need to free one's mind.

There are, of course, some downsides to being creative in one's thinking. One of the most irritating of these, for me, is the suspicion that it engenders in people if they consider that you are being too open. I have come across this mind-set on a number of occasions. However, the upside is clearly greater by many orders of magnitude, and consistency and results ultimately speak for themselves.

K.S. Wong, CEO of Sembcorp Industries, the leading engineering services business in Singapore and living proof of the power of lateral thinking, has employed a high degree of force to create change and progress in the merger of two companies (Singapore Technologies Industrial Corporation and Sembawang Corporation) that have powered their way to the forefront of Asian business.

K.S. told me, early on in my career as an entrepreneur, that "changing the way you think is as important as change itself." This advice remains etched in my brain, and should serve as your final thought.

Exercises

Dispense with titles

Make sure that your company dispenses with titles. That's right, just get rid of all the titles on name cards and stationery. Sure, you need to comply with the legal requirements, but beyond that just ignore all the usual trappings of corporate life and treat everyone like they are a founder or vice-president.

Go one step further, and allow your teams to wear casual clothes to work. Forget about the ban on jeans and sneakers. Encourage your people to express themselves. This is not simply a token gesture, but a recognition that substance is more important than form.

Finally, put aside an afternoon every now and again to listen to colleagues whom you may not speak with very often. Listen to what they have to say about the company and its direction. I can guarantee that you will be surprised by what you learn, and even though the surprises may not always be pleasant, you will certainly benefit from hearing their perspectives.

At techpacific.com I have tried whenever possible to follow my own advice about listening to my colleagues, and in the period from April to September 2000, when we experienced an incredible surge of growth, I found that the most common message from these listening sessions was that we needed to continue to try hard at communicating simple issues. The lesson here is that no matter how great we might think we are at communicating, the reality of a growing organization is that we will never be perfect.

This book

This book is all about freeing your mind. Read it, and let me know of anything I have missed — help me to free my mind as well.

Apple Computer and Chiat Day

One of my constant inspirations since I started working has been the story of Apple Computer and (for most of that time) its "insanely great" products. I never cease to be amazed by their creative work, but if I were to choose one particular example, I would direct people to the seminal "1984" ad which launched the Macintosh, and which (for many people) launched the age of the personal computer.

Visit www.chiatday.com/product/historical work/tv/1984/1984.html and celebrate the birth of the industry that has ultimately made much of the technology revolution possible. The story of the ad is on the main screen, and a link at the bottom allows you to download the whole version.

Sometimes, we need visual aids to help us understand how powerful lateral thought can be, and the Apple ads (including "Think Different") are great aids in that respect.

Once upon a time ...

Writing this book and being one of the founders of techpacific.com is like a dream come true for me. As I have stated, this is still very much in progress, but it all started when I opened my mind beyond the limits of my experience.

There are very few investment bankers who don't at some stage contemplate leaving their firm and setting up on their own, and I have to admit to having this same fantasy for as long as I can remember. I only got the guts to do so in 1998 when I opened my mind and realized that the limits I had been feeling were nothing more than an illusory barrier.

I have to thank Nomura Securities for helping me to take advantage of the situation when they decided to close down the Asian division of the Global Markets Division where I worked in 1998. This decision, taken in the wake of huge losses in the real estate business of Nomura in New York, helped to liberate me from the shackles of my self-imposed exile in the land of corporate slavedom.

Being made redundant from my job at Nomura was the immediate catalyst for starting techpacific.com. Like most investment bankers, my first thought was to look for a similar job, and although the concept of techpacific.com had been brewing for some time, I felt that I could still invest capital in techpacific.com while holding down a full-time job.

Being made redundant certainly challenged my self-esteem for a while, and given that I am just as human as the next person, there was a time when I wondered if I was cut out for entrepreneurship. However, (luckily!) my period of self-doubt was just a passing phase, and like many others who have taken the first steps down this path, I realized that I would have to free my mind and allow myself to think in ways that would normally seem unconventional. When I think back to those days, I'm challenged and inspired anew to continue to think openly and without fear of the consequence. After all, what's the cost of a thought?

In most cases, rising to the challenge of thinking "out of the box" isn't easy. It requires a thick skin and the confidence to stick to the course you have adopted. But the times we live in are unusual in many respects, and getting the most out of your life as an entrepreneur could be the most rewarding thing you can do in your career!

For many of you out there nurturing your own dreams, the catalyst for creating change could be something equally as dramatic and unexpected as it was for me. When that change happens, just be sure to grab the opportunity that comes along with it, and ride the wave to a new life as the technology revolution unfolds in Asia.

Conclusion

I have to admit to a tinge of sadness in writing this conclusion, since it means that I have completed the book, and I have really enjoyed the experience of getting *Underdogs in Overdrive* published!

I would like to take this opportunity to reiterate my own hope of what *Underdogs in Overdrive* represents for me.

As I think I have already stated, I certainly don't consider myself to have yet been successful enough or around long enough as an entrepreneur (though the last two years certainly feels like a lot longer sometimes) to be able to be seen as some sort of shining example of "how to succeed." God knows that we are still at the very early stages of our development in techpacific.com – and success for me is still a case of making more correct calls than mistakes. There are many, many other people who have achieved enough in their careers to be able to write the kind of book that inspires by example.

Neither is this book a history of techpacific.com. I certainly intend to write a short history when we have enough of a track record under our belt, but *Underdogs in Overdrive* is not that book.

It is my hope that this book will serve to inspire entrepreneurs who are based here in Asia with a set of references and guidelines that are relevant to them in this wonderful and exciting time that we are lucky enough to be living in. This environment is absolutely unique, and represents an inflection point in history that will be obvious in years to come. If, as a result of this book, I can have laid claim to even one person successfully jumping into technopreneurship, then I will have more than achieved my aim.

I also hope the book will inspire a new set of business writing that is both "Asian" and "Tech" oriented. Maybe in the next few years, the shelves will not only be full of books on Apple, Microsoft, Intel, Kleiner Perkins, etc, but will also contain a fair share of Asian originated success stories. If I can succeed even somewhat in this area, then it will all have been worth the effort.

In addition to the book, I have set up a website, www.underdogsinoverdrive.com. This will initially be a set of brief resources that relate to the book, but I hope that it will also become an interactive forum for feedback and community use. A short summary of the book, and a short flash animation that is quite good fun, are also available on the website.

Finally, a reminder that my email address is ilyas@techpacific.com. I am quite serious in my invitation to anyone who wants to contact me or ask me any questions to please do so. I cannot promise an immediate reply, but I am generally quite good at getting back to people, so if you do send me an electronic message, then hang in there — I will reply. I am especially interested in your feedback (good or bad) on the ten ideas, and any "true stories" that you think will help to highlight a particular idea. I will set up a section of the website devoted to critical feedback on what ideas work and what doesn't, so please help me get started by sending me your feedback.

Appendix A
Practical pointers for getting funded

This appendix explains how to get the entrepreneurial ball rolling by getting that all-important initial funding. Although I hope you will find useful the pointers set out here, remember that they are just that — *pointers*.

This book is all about creating a set of values, or a manifesto, that will help you to create a great business. With those values, and with great ideas (which you'll have to supply yourself, of course!) you will be successful. Of course, luck will play a part, along with being able to write good business plans and to access the capital that you need. The luck part you'll have to rely upon yourself.

Who provides finance?

At techpacific.com, we frequently come across entrepreneurs who try to convince us that "capital is a commodity" and that there are a ton of people who are ready to write that first check. While it might have been easy at times to raise money, talk is very cheap, and the way in which market sentiment can change has been amply demonstrated following the market crash of spring 2000. In my experience, capital is a scarce and valuable resource, and your pursuit of equity should be taken very seriously.

As I have tried to show, there are some great things that are happening out there with venture capitalists and investors coming into the region. However, knowing someone who can open the doors is still, unfortunately, a prerequisite for most young companies, despite the efforts of people and firms like techpacific.com!

The people you could approach for funding include:

- **Venture capitalists**. Until recently, venture capitalists were a rare breed in Asia, but they are growing in number and diversity. There are local, regional, and international players that have set up shop, mostly in Hong Kong and Singapore, such as Draper Fisher Jurveston, Carlyle Group, J.H. Whitney, and GE Capital. Appendix C lists some of the more prominent and adventurous firms. I can't promise that they will be open to straight start-up finance, nor can I promise that they will be easy to approach, but my advice is that if you have a great idea, go ahead and contact them with a direct call or email.
- **Commercial and retail banks**. Have you ever tried to get venture capital from a banker? Try growing corn on Queens Road Central, in Hong Kong — you might be luckier. The truth is that getting risk capital for

technology from banks isn't a very fruitful pastime, so I wouldn't hold out much hope unless you have some sort of exceptional reason for trying. If you do get past the front door, the likelihood is that they will ask for security, and if, like most early-stage business people, you don't have much security, then you'll quickly appreciate my comments above. Again, however, if you have few alternatives, don't be afraid to go and talk to them. At minimum, you might benefit from their recommendations.

- **Other financial institutions**, such as insurance companies or mutual funds. These guys are getting there, but are most likely to invest in mature businesses and not in start-ups. I have included in the list in Appendix C some of the more obvious firms who finance technology, but the list comes with a huge health warning: these people don't respond well to cold calls and unsolicited business plans. Some individual fund managers might be more receptive to raw start-ups and/or cold calls, and if that's the case when you apply, then good luck. Otherwise, you might be better off waiting until you have some sort of track record.
- **Angels**. God bless them, one and all. Angels are the most likely source of start-up capital. Friends, relatives, colleagues, ex-colleagues, and former school-mates are an important and vastly underrated source of capital for entrepreneurs who are starting out. Some of the

best names in the business started life being funded by angels in some form or another, and I would suggest that you place this source of capital very high on your list. In starting techpacific.com, we relied upon our own angels.

- **Corporate investors**. If your idea fits, you might just strike it lucky, but the chances are that you won't find out in the first place unless you are one of the lucky few that have access to decision-makers. By this, I mean that it's rare to find someone in a large corporation who can take a decision to invest in a start-up, so if you find yourself in the right place at the right time, and a corporation is willing to invest in you when you are setting up shop, then you should take full advantage of this help. Asian corporations that are dominated by family have both a good and a bad side to their investment appetite for technology, and I would be a supporter in general of trying to get some feedback, at least, if you have access to large businesses. In addition to locally based corporations, of course, virtually all the leading technology firms have a presence in most of the capital cities of Asia, and if you have any kind of access to these firms (perhaps through friends working there), then you should go ahead and try them out.

All of the large names, such as Microsoft, Intel, Yahoo, Lycos, and Cisco, have their Asian contacts available from their websites. In addition, I have included a few in Appendix C.

Appendix B

Guidelines for creating a business plan

Getting in front of an investor is obviously a big part of the story, but another important hurdle in getting investors to part with their cash is the production of a business plan.

I have a deep-seated dislike and mistrust of "cookie cutter" business plans, and most of my colleagues will confirm that in setting up techpacific.com I avoided producing anything that was "conventional" in the sense of a 100-page dissertation, which is what some venture capital firms still expect.

Of course, once a firm has been established, and the entrepreneur has attracted outside capital and has a team of people in place, they will need to start thinking about how to describe their vision when they start moving forward and have to raise more serious amounts of capital. It's only to be expected that investors will then demand some sort of business plan that they can "sign off" on. As the business grows, and along with it the amount of capital that's raised, business plans serve an essential and more sophisticated role in creating and maintaining a tool for accountability.

Having said that, I would be the first to admit that there is a role even in early stage companies for a summary document that is clearly written, concise, and informative. Since I haven't managed to come up with a new term that might describe such a document, I'm afraid that we'll have to resort to using the term "business plan."

Most intelligent investors will understand the limitations that a start-up faces, and won't expect the depth and breadth in a business plan for seed or series A capital that they would expect from a pre-IPO or even an IPO company. (If you would like to see what is expected in an IPO, you are welcome to contact me and I'll send you a copy of our IPO document.)

So, what is this document that we will call a business plan? In very crude terms, a business plan is created to explain to a third party (most often an investor, but sometimes also a partner or potential employee) what the business actually does. In addition, the plan helps people to understand and appreciate the potential of the business, what the entrepreneur plans to do over a given period of time, and how the company intends to execute its plans.

A good business plan also acts as an extended resume for the founder and his or her key staff, since investors will usually base a large part of their decision for early stage investing on their assessment of the management team.

Finally, the business plan will help to create an understanding of the financial dynamics of the proposed venture. In most cases, this aspect of the plan is the one that gets most worked over again and again by investors who are serious about committing capital. I believe that as long as the entrepreneur tries to cover as many bases as possible, and to show that they have thought carefully about the costs of starting the business and the potential size of the market, then they will be in good shape. Covering many bases means that the financial plan should incorporate as many market-related assumptions as possible. Investors like to see that the entrepreneur has catered for changes in circumstances outside their control. I have found that even if I disagree with the analysis, I'm willing to give high marks to an entrepreneur who can show that they have thought about external factors.

It's important to realize that investors receive many, many business plans each month, and so quality and clarity of writing is crucial to ensure that your business plan is read favorably. I would go as far as saying that if you can't write well, then it's worthwhile having your plan read over for style and consistency by someone you trust. If this person is a professional writer or an experienced consultant, then so much the better. However, remember: style will rarely win out over substance. In my experience at techpacific.com, some of the greatest businesses aren't those with the best-written business plans from a stylistic standpoint, but rather those that present their ideas innovatively and represent ideas that have panache.

I have created two types of informational template for those of you who might want a more proactive helping hand in writing a business plan. First is a summary outline of a plan with the various sections numbered on the left of the table, followed by a description of the purpose of the section, and then some indication of the number of pages that this section might require. The result is a typical outline for a business plan consisting of between ten and fifteen pages of information which will present sufficient detail for investors to make an initial assessment on whether to seek further information on which to base a decision to invest.

I have then elaborated on the summary outline by filling in the content of a fictional business plan. It's a very short summary, and I would urge you to read and digest both sections in order to get a better sense of the way in which a real plan might work.

Additional comments appear in bold type at the end of most sections.

A typical summary

Section	Purpose	Length (pages)
1. **Executive Summary**	A concise summary of the entire business plan	1–2
2. **Company Description** • Background/History • Capital structure/ Shareholders' list	Background information about the company, including capital structure if relevant. Explain why you started the firm, and include a description of the "vision."	1–2
3. **Product/Service** • Description • Technology • Benefit to customers	What will the company provide its customers? How will customers benefit from the company's products/services compared to what they currently use/have?	1–3
4. **Market Analysis** • Size • Geographic focus • Growth • Customer profile	How many potential customers of the company are there? What is their growth rate? What is the estimated share of the market the company plans to capture? How can the company find and approach customers?	1–2
5. **Analysis of Competition** • Existing competition • Substitute products/ services • SWOT (Strength/Weakness/ Opportunity/Threat) analysis • Competitive advantages • Barriers to entry	Who are the company's competitors? In what areas is the company stronger/weaker than its competitors? Are there barriers to entry (e.g. technology/regulatory) that can prevent others entering the market?	1–2
6. **Execution of Business Plan** • Strategy • Alliances • Implementation timetable and budget	How will the business plan be implemented? What are the strategies and tactics of the company?	1–3

A typical summary (continued)

Section	Purpose	Length (pages)
7. **Management Team** • Short biographies of founders and key members	Who are the people in the company? What experience, track record, and expertise do they bring to the company? This is a critical part of the plan. Many investors move directly to this section before reading anything else. Provide credible references. Many people attach a formal appendix with resumes.	1–2 (Half a page per person unless you have lots of people in the key team slots)
8. **Capital Requirements** • Amount required • Valuation and its justification • Use of proceeds	How much does the company require to implement the business plan? How does the company value itself to external investors? What is the expected "burn rate" (or money spent per month)?	1–2
9. **Financial Analysis** • Projected profit and loss • Cash flow	Financial projections of the company. This section is often an appendix to the main body of the plan. It's often the section most changed if an investor is interested enough to go forward with due diligence.	1–3

A fictional business plan for XYZ Company Limited

Section 1: Executive summary

(1–2 pages)

I wish to build a company that will cut by 75% the time it takes to transmit wireless signals across crowded cityscapes. I will do this by engineering neural networks that contain packets of data that can float free and be stored away from traditional silicon confines.

These networks will mean that lasers can be more efficiently deployed.

Section 2: Brief history of XYZ

(1–2 pages)

The company was established in August 2000, and is incorporated in Hong Kong. I am the company's sole director, and the company secretary is ABC Lawyers who also established the entity.

I researched the idea of neural networks over the past three years at university, and then when I was working at a laser deployment facility and research laboratory in Shanghai.

The brief history of my company is as follows:

[Discuss the paid-up capital, incorporation and business registration details, the directors, give a breakdown of the shareholders, etc.]

Section 3: Our products and services

(1–3 pages)

My product will be used by any company or organization that depends on the transmission of data.

It will be of special interest to companies that have "rich media," and who are interested in wireless transmission.

These companies will buy my product because it is cheaper and faster than any currently available alternative.

My product will be distributed by the large incumbent telcos, who need to have a broader range of services.

My product will provide the distributors with better services and a new source of income.

[It's important to elaborate upon each of the sentences summarised above. You will want the reader to be able to leave this section having a pretty clear understanding of how the product was created and what market opportunity it meets.]

Section 4: Market analysis

(1–2 pages)

I believe that my product has a global applicability. However, it is of special interest in any large metropolitan area in Asia. My target markets are therefore Mumbai, Bangkok, Singapore, Kuala Lumpur, Jakarta, Beijing, Shanghai, Hong Kong, Seoul, Tokyo, Osaka, Manila, and Taipei.

The target consumer/customer base is multi-million in Asia alone.

I have assumed that each transmission will generate a micro-payment and that each license to a large telco will result in a license fee. I also assume that any data owner that uses my service will pay a fee to the telco, and my company will have a revenue share agreement.

The key clients I have targeted are:

[Many entrepreneurs forget that market data is easy to access off the Internet. The websites of companies such as Cisco (www.cisco.com), Nortel (www.nortel.com), and IBM (www.ibm.com) are wonderful resources for data of

many kinds. In addition, there is a wealth of information and data available from magazines such as *Red Herring* (www.redherring.com), *Wired* (www.wired.com) and *Industry Standard* (www.thestandard.com). Prospective investors will certainly do their own diligence on the size and scope of the market, but being provided with authoritative data will be a plus point.]

Section 5: The competition

(1–2 pages)

The competitive landscape is DSL and optical network managers. These are companies such as Bell South, ATT, HarvardNet, and HK Telecom.

I believe that my company is able to deal with this pressure due to:

- Reason A
- Reason B
- Reason C
- Reason D

[No one ever gets high marks for assuming that there are no competitors. There is always competition, and you should be careful to acknowledge these threats and use the opportunity to explain why you will be successful.]

Section 6: Implementation strategy

(1–3 pages)

My business plan will be implemented in two phases:

1. product testing and field trials; and
2. full-scale deployment.

In order to achieve these phases, I will need US$100 million raised in three stages.

My management team is already assembled. It consists of Mr. Smith, Ms Jones, and Professor Chan.

I have signed agreements with NASA for initial field trials.

My product will be manufactured in Taipei. I have preliminary agreements and prototypes that can be viewed with Prototype Ltd in Taiwan.

[This section is the second most important of the whole business plan, after the section on the management team. No investor will commit serious capital until and unless they are convinced that the company will be able to implement its plan. The difference between "cheap" talk and multi-million dollar success is mostly the implementation of the business plan.]

Section 7: Management team

(1–2 pages)

My management team bio-data in full is included hereunder.

References are available on request.

[It's often best to contain some sort of write-up of the management team that can bring to life the relevance of their experience and the dynamism that they bring to the table. I recommend putting the formal resumes in an appendix.]

Section 8: Funding requirements

(1–2 pages)

I require US$5 million in this fundraising round. My company valuation is set at US$15 million pre-money.

I have based this valuation on various analyses:

- Comparables (see table below showing companies in the US, Japan, Korea, and Singapore that are comparable).
- My business plan shows the returns that are contained in section 9 below. You will see that the total returns to current investors could be 40% p.a. over five years.
- I have an indication from an existing company that they would be prepared to invest in my company at a valuation of US$5 million.

I will use the capital as follows (see below).

[This is another vital section. If the numbers don't make sense, and the use of proceeds from any investment or fundraising exercise isn't clearly set out, then the proposition will suffer. Be clear, be upfront with your expectations, and don't be emotive.]

Section 9: Financial data

(1–3 pages)

Please find below a full set of financial projections and historic numbers. You can call my CFO on (890) 123344 or email him at iopak@ronclioen.com if you require further information.

Appendix C

List of venture capital firms

Company	Telephone	Fax	Address	Website
3i Asia	65 438 3131	65 536 2429	#17-02 The Exchange 20 Cecil Street Singapore 049705	www.3ius.com
ABN AMRO	852 2868 0368	852 2147 2939	40/F, Cheung Kong Center 2 Queen's Road Central Hong Kong	www.abnamro.com.hk
AC Ventures	603 7952 4800	603 7958 2210	AMCORP Trade Centre 18, Persiaran Barat Off Jalan Timur 46050 Petaling Jaya Selangor Darul Ehsan Malaysia	www.ac-ventures.com
Active Capital Asia	65 248 4702	65 248 4960	80 Raffles Place UOB Plaza 1 #35-00 Singapore 048624	www.activecapitalasia.com
Advanced Multimedia Group, Inc. (Hong Kong, China)	852 2815 4020	852 2815 4021	10b Dotcom House 128 Wellington Street Central, Hong Kong	www.amginternational.com
Advent International Corp	852 2978 9300	852 2826 9247	Suite 808, Alexandra House 16–20 Chater Road Central, Hong Kong	www.adventinternational.com

Company	Telephone	Fax	Address	Website
American Pacific Techno-logy Group	852 2960 4611	852 2960 0185	21/F, Westlands Centre 20 Westlands Road Quarry Bay, Hong Kong	www.aptgnet.com
Asia Alliance	852 2236 7777	852 2236 7888	39/F, One Pacific Place 88 Queensway Hong Kong	www.asialliance.com
AsiaCommerce (North Asia)	852 3102 8600	852 3102 9002	Suite 707, Edinburgh Tower The Landmark, 15 Queen's Road Central, Hong Kong	www.asiacommerce.com
Asia Debt Management HK Ltd	852 2536 4567	852 2147 2813	907, Asia Pacific Finance Tower 3 Garden Road Central, Hong Kong	www.asiadebt.com
AsiaTech Ventures Limited	852 2116 6868	852 2116 0000	2308 Alexandra House 18 Chater Road Central, Hong Kong	www.asiatechv.com
BancBoston Capital	852 2867 7687	852 2521 0798	8/F, Jardine House 1 Connaught Place Central, Hong Kong	www.bancbostonventures.com
Baring Private Equity Partners (Hong Kong) Ltd	852 2843 9329	852 2843 9372	39/F, One International Finance Centre 1 Harbour View Street Central, Hong Kong	www.bpep.com
Beijing Venture Capital Co., Ltd	8610 6894 3739	8610 6894 3779	10/F, Haidian Science Technology Tower No. A7 Baishiqiao Road, Haidian District Beijing 100081 China	www.bvcc.com.cn

Company	Telephone	Fax	Address	Website
Brierley	65 438 0002	65 435 0100	20 Collyer Quay #16-02/03, Tung Centre Singapore 049317	www.bilgroup.com
Camerlin	603 925 1933	603 925 1932	Level 9, Wisma Hong Leong 18 Jalan Perak, 50450 Kuala Lumpur, Malaysia	N/A
Canton Venture Capital Co. Ltd	8620 8755 6020	8620 8755 6023	11/F, Metro Plaza 183 North Tianhe Road Guangzhou 510075 China	www.c-vcc.com
Carlyle Asia – HK	852 2878 7000	852 2878 7007	32/F, Asia Pacific Finance Tower 3 Garden Road Central, Hong Kong	www.thecarlylegroup.com
	813 5219 1249	813 5219 1413	15/F, East Tower, Otemachi First Square 1-5-1 Otemachi, Chiyoda-ku Tokyo 100-0004 Japan	
CDC Capital Partners	65 232 2766	65 232 2889	Level 15, Prudential Tower 30 Cecil Street Singapore 049712	www.cdcgroup.com
Chase Capital Partners	852 2533 1818		30/F, One International Finance Centre 1 Harbour View Street Central, Hong Kong	www.chasecapital.com
	1212 899 3400	1212 899 3401	1221 Avenue of the Americas New York, NY 10020 United States	

Company	Telephone	Fax	Address	Website
China Resources Investment Management Co., Ltd	8610 6510 2718	8610 6510 2722	712 Office Tower, 1 Bright China Chang An Bldg. No. 7 Jian Guomen Nei Avenue Beijing 100005 China	www.crim.com.cn
Chinadotcom	852 2893 8200	852 2571 2120	20/F, Citicorp Centre 18 Whitfield Road Causeway Bay, Hong Kong	www.china.com
ChinaVest Ltd	852 2810 7081	852 2845 2949	19/F, Dina House 11 Duddell Street Central, Hong Kong	www.chinavest.com
Cisco Systems (HK) Ltd	852 2588 3100	852 2588 3299	31/F, Great Eagle Centre 23 Harbour Road Wanchai, Hong Kong	www.cisco.com
	65 833 5500	65 833 5599	501 Orchard Road #10-00 Wheelock Place Singapore 238880	
	1408 526 4000		170 West Tasman Drive San Jose, CA 95134 United States	
Citicorp Capital Asia	886 2717 9421	886 2718 0037	N/A	www.citibank.com
Credit Suisse First Boston	852 2101 6000	852 2101 7990	22/F, Three Exchange Square Central, Hong Kong	www.csfb.com

Company	Telephone	Fax	Address	Website
Daum Communications Corp.	822 550 9800	822 550 9891	154–8 Samsung-dong, Kangnam-gu Seoul, Korea	www.daum.net
Dell Ventures	800 601 1054 (Toll Free)	65 335 3380	180 Clemenceau Avenue, #06-01 Haw Par Centre Singapore 239922	www.dellventures.com
Dragon Tech Venture	852 2801 7333	852 2899 2711	23/F, Chekiang First Bank Centre 1 Duddell Street Central, Hong Kong	www.dragontechventures.com
Draper Fisher Jurvetson	1650 599 9000	1650 599 9726	Suit 250, 400 Seaport Court Redwood City, CA 94063 United States	www.drapervc.com
	852 2536 3996	852 2537 0779	Suite 3106, One Exchange Square Central, Hong Kong	
Dresdner Kleinwert Benson Ltd	852 2238 8888	852 2845 9003	21/F, Cheung Kong Center 2 Queen's Road Central Hong Kong	www.dresdnerkb.com
E.M. Warburg, Pincus & Co. Asia, Ltd	852 2521 3183	852 2521 3869	12/F, St. George's Building 2 Ice House Street Central, Hong Kong	www.warburgpincus.com
Emerging Markets Partnership (H.K.) Ltd	852 2918 7999	852 2572 3663	Suites 1201–1202, Two Pacific Place 88 Queensway Hong Kong	www.empwdc.com

Company	Telephone	Fax	Address	Website
Enron Asia Pacific	800 808 0363		P.O. Box 1188 Houston, TX 77251–1188 United States	www.enron.com
ESamsung China	8610 6566 9416	8610 6566 9389	28/F, China Merchants Tower No. 2, Dong Huan Nan Lu Chao Yang District Beijing 100022 China	www.esamsung.com
Fidelity Ventures Hong Kong	852 2629 2800	852 2509 0371	17/F, One International Finance Centre 1 Harbour View Street Central, Hong Kong	www.fidelityventures.com
GE Capital	852 2100 6700	852 2100 6733	16/F, Three Exchange Square Central, Hong Kong	www.gecapital.com
GEMS	852 2838 0093	852 2838 0292	2108 Gloucester Tower The Landmark, 11 Pedder Street Central, Hong Kong	www.gem.com.hk
General Atlantic Partners	852 2166 8749	852 2166 8999	18/F, One International Finance Centre 1 Harbour View Street Central, Hong Kong	www.gapartners.com
GIC	65 337 3303	65 330 6891	331 North Bridge Road #09-10/06 Odeon Towers Singapore 188720	www.gic.com.sg
Goldman Sachs	852 2978 1000	852 2978 0440	68/F, Cheung Kong Centre 2 Queen's Road Central Hong Kong	www.gs.com

Company	Telephone	Fax	Address	Website
Guangdong Technology Venture Capital Co. Ltd	8620 8761 8523 8620 8761 3876	8620 8761 2766	13/F, Hi-Tech R&D Center, Xianile Road Guangzhou, China	www.gtvc.com
Guoco	852 2218 8888	852 2285 3888	73/F, The Centre 99 Queen's Road Central Hong Kong	www.guoco.com
HarbourVest	852 2525 2214	852 2525 2241	Suite 1207, Citibank Tower 3 Garden Road Central, Hong Kong	www.harbourvest.com
Hatchasia.com	65 446 4847 65 441 9983	65 441 9661	Suite 3, 750A Chai Chee Road, #07-02 Technopark at Chai Chee Singapore 469001	www.hatchasia.com
Hendale Asia Asia Group	852 2840 0776	852 2840 0557	22/F, Entertainment Building 30 Queen's Road Central Hong Kong	www.hendale.com
Henderson Cyber Ltd.	852 2908 8818	852 2868 1028	6/F, World-Wide House 19 Des Voeux Road Central Hong Kong	www.hendersoncyber.com
HSBC Private Equity Technology Ltd	852 2822 1111	852 2810 1112	GPO Box 64, Hong Kong 1 Queen's Road Central Hong Kong	www.hsbc.com
Ibusiness	852 2126 3333	852 2121 8111	12/F, Cheung Kong Center, 2 Queen's Road Central Hong Kong	www.ibusiness-hk.com

Company	Telephone	Fax	Address	Website
IDG Technology Venture Investment Inc., Headquarters	8610 6526 2400	8610 6526 0700	Rm 616, Tower A, COFCO 8 Jianguomen Nei Dajie Beijing 100005 China	www.ptvchina.com
Incubasia Ltd	852 2285 8181	852 2285 8383	1501, CEF Life Tower 248 Queen's Road East Hong Kong	www.incubasia.com
Indochina Asset Management Ltd	848 824 1234	848 824 1122	Ho Chi Minh City Vietnam	www.icaminvest.com
Intel Semiconductor Ltd **Intel Capital**	852 2844 4555	852 2868 1989	32/F, Two Pacific Place 88 Queensway Hong Kong	www.intel.com/capital
internet.com Corporation	1212 547 7900	1212 953 1733	3/F, 501 5th Avenue New York, NY 10017 United States	www.internet.comvc.com
Itochu	852 2861 9877	852 2527 2290	28/F, United Centre 95 Queensway Hong Kong	www.itochu.com
	813 3497 7295	813 3497 7296	5-1, Kita-Aoyama, 2-Chome, Minato-Ku Tokyo 107-8077 Japan	
Jafco	852 2536 1960	852 2536 1979	20/F, Asia Pacific Finance Tower Citibank Plaza, 3 Garden Road Central, Hong Kong	www.jafcoasia.com
	813 5223 7536	813 5223 7561	Tekko Building, 1-8-2 Marunouchi, Chiyoda-ku Tokyo 100-0005 Japan	

Company	Telephone	Fax	Address	Website
Jump Start Incubator	852 2237 7700	852 2806 8046	31/F, Citicorp Centre 18 Whitfield Road Causeway Bay, Hong Kong	www.jumpstartasia.com
Kerry Holding Ltd	852 2525 7211	852 2869 9563	21/F, Citic Tower 1 Tim Mei Avenue Central, Hong Kong	N/A
Kuwait Fund for Arab Economic Development	965 246 8800	965 241 9060	PO Box 2921 Safat 13030 Kuwait	www.kuwait-fund.org
LabMorgan	65 362 9412	65 326 9919	6 Shenton Way #32-08 DBS Building Tower Two Singapore 0688091	www.labmorgan.com
Lombard	1415 397 5900	1415 397 5820	36/F, 600 Montgomery Street San Francisco, CA 94111 United States	www.lombardinvestments.com
Macquarie Bank	612 8232 3333	612 8232 3350	1 Martin Place Sydney NSW 2000 Australia	www.macquarie.com.au
	852 2823 3700	852 2823 3790	17/F, Citic Tower, 1 Tim Mei Avenue Central, Hong Kong	
Merrill Lynch	852 2536 3888	852 2536 3281	17/F, Asia Pacific Finance Tower 3 Garden Road Central, Hong Kong	www.merrilllynch.com
Microsoft Hong Kong Limited	852 2804 4250	852 2560 2217	20/F, Citiplaza Three 14 Taikoo Wan Road Quarry Bay, Hong Kong	www.microsoft.com.hk

Company	Telephone	Fax	Address	Website
Morgan Stanley Dean Witter Asia	852 2848 5200	852 2848 1012	30/F, Three Exchange Square Central, Hong Kong	www.msdw.com
Morningside Asia	852 2894 9800	852 2577 3509	22/F, Hang Lung Centre 2–20 Paterson Street Causeway Bay, Hong Kong	www.morningsidetech.com
Netalone.com	852 2330 0336	852 2296 6966	68/F, The Center 99 Queen's Road Central Hong Kong	www.netalone.com
News Digital Ventures	852 2621 8888	852 2621 9624	15/F, One Harbourfront 18 Tak Fung Street, Hunghom Kowloon, Hong Kong	www.newscorp.com
New World Cyberbase	852 2138 8000	852 2138 8067	37/F, New World Tower 16–18 Queen's Road Central Hong Kong	www.nwcyberbase.com
Nortel Networks	852 2100 2888	852 2100 2710	27/F, Citiplaza One, 111 King's Road Quarry Bay, Hong Kong	www.nortelnetworks.com
NSTB	65 779 7066	65 773 2795	10 Science Park Road #01-01/03 The Alpha Singapore Science Park II Singapore 117684	www.nstb.gov.sg
Orchid Asia Holdings	1415 875 5600	1415 781 2189	Suite 51870, 555 California Street San Francisco, CA 94104-1716 United States	www.orchidasia.com

Company	Telephone	Fax	Address	Website
Pacific Century CyberWorks – Main Offices	852 2514 8888	852 2524 4375	38/F, Citibank Tower Citibank Plaza, 3 Garden Road Central, Hong Kong	www.cyberworks.com
Pacific Venture	8622 2509 3533	8622 2509 9358	5/F, No. 420 Fu Hsin N Road, Taipei, Taiwan	www.pacificventuregroup.com
PPM Ventures (Asia) Limited	852 2868 5330		Suites 1213–19, Two Pacific Place 88 Queensway, Hong Kong	www.ppmventures.com
Prudential Asset Management Asia HK Ltd	852 2844 1000	852 2877 3748	32/F, Alexandra House 18 Chater Road Central, Hong Kong	www.prudential.com
Regent Pacific Private Equity Limited	852 2514 6110	852 2509 3640	904–906 Asia Pacific Finance Tower 3 Garden Road Central, Hong Kong	www.regentpac.com
iregent	852 2514 6111	852 2810 4396	904–906 Asia Pacific Finance Tower Citibank Plaza 3 Garden Road Central, Hong Kong	www.iregentgroup.com
Reuters Venture Capital	4420 7542 9397	4420 7542 4363	85 Fleet Street London, EC4P 4AJ, United Kingdom	www.rvcco.com
Shanghai Information Investment Inc.	8621 6207 7002	8621 6207 7001	1318 Beijing Road (W) Shanghai 200040 China	www.sii.com.cn

Company	Telephone	Fax	Address	Website
Softbank China Venture Capital	86 21 3212 4666	86 21 5240 0366	28/F, Zhao Feng World Trade Building 369 Jiang Su Road Shanghai 200050 China	www.sbcvc.com/sbcvce
Sunevision		852 2802 0022	21/F, Sun Hung Kai Centre 30 Harbour Road Wanchai, Hong Kong	www.sunevision.com
Telecom Venture Group Limited	852 2147 2080	852 2147 3320	Suite 3810, Jardine House 1 Connaught Place Central, Hong Kong	www.tvgfunds.com
Tinshed Hong Kong	852 2526 9821	852 2845 8175	1408 Prince's Building, 10 Chater Road Central, Hong Kong	www.tinshed.com
	612 8356 2900	612 8356 2999	351 Crown Street Surry Hills, NSW 2010 Australia	
United Overseas Bank Ltd	65 533 9898	65 534 2334	5/F, 80 Raffles Place UOB Plaza 2 Singapore 048624	www.uob.com.sg
Vertex Management (II) Pte. Ltd	852 2523 6133	852 2523 7233	63/FB, Bank of China Tower 1 Garden Road Central, Hong Kong	www.vertexmgt.com
	65 777 0122	65 777 1878	77 Science Park Drive #02-15 Cintech III Singapore Science Park Singapore 118256	

Company	Telephone	Fax	Address	Website
Viventures	65 838 9570	65 838 9569	3 Temasek Avenue #30-03 Centennial Tower Singapore 039190	www.viventures.com
VL Neuberg Capital Ltd	852 2919 5350	852 2802 8229	Room 1707, 17/F, Central Plaza 18 Harbour Road Central, Hong Kong	www.vlneuberg.com
Walden International Investment Group (WIIG)	852 2523 0615	852 2521 5778	Suites 1203–1211 12/F, Two Pacific Place 88 Queensway Hong Kong	www.wiig.com/main
Warburg Pincus	852 2521 3183	852 2521 3869	12/F, St. George's Building 2 Ice House Street Central, Hong Kong	www.warburgpincus.com
Whitney Asia Ltd	852 2110 7980	852 2111 9699	Suite 2705, Citibank Tower 3 Garden Road Central, Hong Kong	www.jhwhitney.com
WI Harper Beijing Management Consultant Co. Ltd	852 2151 8128	852 2151 8138	Suite 2914, One International Finance Centre 1 Harbour View Streetadd Central, Hong Kong	www.wiharper.com

Index

G

H

I

J

K

L

M

N

O

P

R

S

T

U

V

W

Y

CUSTOMER NOTE: IF THIS BOOK IS ACCOMPANIED BY SOFTWARE, PLEASE READ THE FOLLOWING BEFORE OPENING THE PACKAGE.

This CD-ROM contains files to complement the accompanying book. By opening the package, you are agreeing to be bound by the following agreement.

This software product is protected by copyright and all rights are reserved by the author, John Wiley & Sons (Asia) Pte Ltd or their licensors. You are licensed to use this software on a single computer. Copying the software to another medium or format for use on a single computer does not violate the U.S. Copyright Law. Copying the software for any other purpose is a violation of the U.S. Copyright Law.

This software product is sold as is without warranty of any kind, either express or implied, including but not limited to the implied warranty of merchantability and fitness for a particular purpose. Neither Wiley nor its dealers or distributors assumes any liability for any alleged or actual damages arising from the use of or the inability to use this software. (Some states do not allow the exclusion of implied warranties, so the exclusion may not apply to you.)